Financial Institutions and Services Series

Global Banking Regulation and Supervision

What are the Issues and what are the Practices?

FINANCIAL INSTITUTIONS AND SERVICES SERIES

Stock Exchanges, IPO's and Mutual funds
E. Klein (Editor)
2004 ISBN: 1-59454-173-6

Global Banking Issues
E. Klein (Editor)
2005 ISBN: 1-59454-172-8

Financial Institutions and Development
E. Klein (Editor)
2005 ISBN: 1-59454-177-9

Capital Formation, Governance and Banking
E. Klein (Editor)
2005 ISBN: 1-59454-191-4

U. S. Coins: The Price of a Penny
Walter M. Carvalho (Editor)
2009 ISBN: 978-1-60692-939-1

Hedge Funds: Regulation and Nonregulation
Yeram E. Torrey (Editor)
2009. ISBN: 978-1-60692-041-1

Reforming Risk in Financial Markets
Melvin R. Turley (Editor)
2009 ISBN: 978-1-60692-445-7

Information Sellers and Resellers
Shane C. Leger (Editor)
2009. ISBN: 978-1-60692-228-6

Econometric Modeling of Value-at-Risk
Timotheos Angelidis and Stavros Degiannakis
2009. ISBN: 978-1-60741-040-9

Liquidity, Interest Rates and Banking
Jeffrey Morrey and Alexander Guyton (Editors)
2009. ISBN: 978-1-60692-775-5

Securitization of Subprime Mortgages
Milton R. Spotgeste (Editor)
2009. ISBN: 978-1-60692-200-2

Global Banking Regulation and Supervision: What are the Issues and What are the Practices?
James R. Baeraath, Jie Gan, and Daniel E. Nolle
2009 ISBN 978-1-60741-315-8

Financial Institutions and Services Series

GLOBAL BANKING REGULATION AND SUPERVISION

WHAT ARE THE ISSUES AND WHAT ARE THE PRACTICES?

JAMES R. BARTH

JIE GAN

AND

DANIEL E. NOLLE

Nova Science Publishers, Inc.

New York

For permission to use material from this book please contact us:
Telephone 631-231-7269; Fax 631-231-8175
Web Site: http://www.novapublishers.com

LIBRARY OF CONGRESS CATALOGING-IN-PUBLICATION DATA

Barth, James R.
Global banking regulation and supervision : what are the issues and what are the practices? / James R. Barth, Jie Gan, and Daniel E. Nolle.
p. cm.
Includes index.
ISBN 978-1-60741-315-8 (softcover)
1. Banks and banking. 2. Financial institutions--Law and legislation. 3. Globalization. I. Gan, Jie. II. Nolle, Daniel E., 1950- III. Title.
HG1615.B3734 2009
354.8'6211--dc22

2009006382

Published by Nova Science Publishers, Inc. † New York

CONTENTS

PREFACE

The past two decades have witnessed both tremendous change and tremendous growth in the financial sector in countries across the globe. At the same time, however, many countries in the world have experienced banking crises, sometimes leading to costly bank failures and overall disruption in economic activity. The changes in the banking landscape and banking crises have focused policy makers' and industry participants' attention on the appropriate role and structure of banking supervision and regulation. As countries make different choices in these regards, it is useful to inquire if there are fundamental principles countries can follow to insure financial system stability and growth. This paper does not presume to outline such principles, but it does take two necessary steps in that direction: first, it identifies basic issues in banking regulation and supervision; and second, it presents information on how countries around the globe have addressed these issues in their bank regulatory and supervisory schemes.

The study draws on recent research and detailed cross-country data, including data from a new World Bank survey of bank regulation and supervision worldwide, to focus on some of the underlying reasons for and implications of developments in a variety of areas. These include the following: the nature and changing role of banks in promoting economic growth, development and stability; restrictions on the scope of banking activities and allowable ownership arrangements in which to conduct them; the structure and scope of bank regulatory and supervisory schemes; supervisory practices to promote safe and sound banks; market discipline and corporate governance in banking; international cooperation in regulation and supervision; offshore banking; potential disputes in banking arising from World Trade Organization membership; and deposit insurance schemes.

Chapter 1

INTRODUCTION

There is a growing and widening acceptance of the view that financial markets are an essential ingredient in promoting economic growth, development, and stability. Countries everywhere are therefore encouraged to do everything possible not to impede the development of financial markets, including the banking system, which is a particularly important component. Banks are instrumental not only in extending credit to finance both consumption and investment projects, but are also the conduit through which monetary policy is conducted, and banks serve as the payment mechanism through which transactions are consummated. Yet, it is clear that the role of banks has been evolving as countries move through various stages of economic development. As countries mature economically the credit role of banks diminishes, while the role of the capital markets becomes more important. This development has contributed to increased competitive pressures on banks, particularly in the economically more advanced countries, which has resulted in consolidation in the banking industry and expansion in the range of products and services banks offer.

The globalization of trade and services has also increased banks' efforts to service customers internationally. This has resulted in a greater number of international banks, which in many cases conduct more business abroad than in their home country. The rapid development of new technology that facilitates the more cost-effective ability to collect and process vast amounts of information, and to communicate anywhere at any time, has also contributed to the changing role of banks with respect to managing their own risks, to distributing their products and services, and to helping customers manage both their wealth and various types of risk.

At the same time that the role of banking has been changing, the way in which banks are regulated and supervised has also been changing.[1] A growing number of countries have recently taken responsibility for bank regulation and supervision away from the central bank and instead placed it in a separate regulatory authority, in some cases one which encompasses securities firms or insurance companies as well as banks. This development has occurred in part because financial conglomerates have become more numerous and offer a variety of financial products and services that cut across different institutional regulatory lines. Countries in which banks have been heavily government owned have also been increasingly privatizing many of them, which in some cases has resulted in mergers and acquisitions involving foreign banks. This too has spurred the internationalization or globalization of banking. These developments raise issues about who should regulate and supervise big international banking and financial conglomerates operating across many national borders, and how such regulation and supervision should be conducted.

The purpose of this paper is to describe and discuss many of the recent global trends in the bank regulatory and supervisory environment, drawing in particular upon a new database compiled by the World Bank. The remainder of the paper proceeds as follows. The second section provides an overview of financial markets and banking systems. This involves a discussion of the importance of finance for growth, the role of banks in economies, the relative importance of banks in financial systems, and what a "bank" is in different countries. The third section focuses on the regulation and supervision of banks. This involves a discussion of who supervises banks, how banks are supervised, market discipline and corporate governance in banking, risk management, cross-border issues, offshore financial centers, and the implications of World Trade Organization (WTO) membership on the prudential regulation and supervision of banks. The fourth section discusses the way in which the features of formal deposit insurance schemes that countries have adopted differ from one another. The last section contains the summary and conclusions.

[1] "Regulation" refers to the set of laws and rules applicable to banking, and "supervision" is defined as the monitoring by authorities of banks' activities and the enforcement of banking regulations. Barth, Nolle, Phumiwasana and Yago (2003, p.70, footnote 7) refer to a line of reasoning that has been developed explaining why banks should not be regulated.

Chapter 2

OVERVIEW OF FINANCIAL MARKETS AND BANKING SYSTEMS

FINANCE AND GROWTH

As Table 1 shows, the high-income group of countries contains only 15 percent of the world's population (921 million people), but account for 81 percent of the world's gross domestic product (GDP). These countries also hold 87 percent of world banking assets, 93 percent of world equity market capitalization, and 97 percent of world bond capitalization. Clearly, this group of countries accounts for the preponderant shares of everything but population.

By extension, the middle- and low-income groups of countries with 85 percent of the world's population (5.2 billion people) account for only 19 percent of the world's GDP. They also hold only 13 percent of world banking assets, 7 percent of world equity market capitalization, and 3 percent of world bond market capitalization. As the table shows, moreover, even in the case of these two income groups with roughly equal populations the shares of world GDP and world financial assets are skewed towards the middle-income countries.

The information in Table 1 unequivocally demonstrates that the financial systems of higher-income countries are significantly larger relative to GDP than those of lower-income countries. Yet, prior to the 1990s, relatively little research was directed to the issues of whether and how the financial system fostered economic growth.[2] The prevailing view was that economic growth leads financial

2 See Levine (1997), Khan (2000), Khan and Senhdj (2000), Wachtel (2003), Caprio and Honohan (2001), and Phumiwasana (2003) for surveys of the literature on the role of the financial system in economic growth. For a comprehensive survey of this literature as well as several other aspects of

sector growth, which responded to the wider and deeper development of markets for goods and services. However, within the last decade, a growing body of research has focused on the possible positive causal connection between the development of the financial system and overall economic development. This literature outlines several key ways in which financial systems contribute to economic growth:

Table 1. Finance and Growth: Wide Disparities in Population, Income and Financial Markets Among Countries

	Total	Percent Accounted for by:		
		High Income Countries	**Middle Income Countries**	**Low Income Countries**
Population	6.1 billion	15.1	43.7	41.1
GDP	$31.1 trillion	80.6	16.0	3.4
Bank Assets	$36.9 trillion	86.6	11.9	1.5
Equity Market Capitalization	$27.8 trillion	92.9	6.6	0.6
Bond Market Capitalization	$31.6 trillion	96.9	2.6	0.6
Total Financial Assets	*$96.4 trillion*	*91.8*	*7.3*	*0.9*

Source: Statistical Abstract of the United States, U.S. Census Bureau; World Development Indicators, World Bank; World Economic Outlook and International Financial Statistics, International Monetary Fund; Emerging Stock Market Factbook, Standard & Poor's and Size of World Bond Market Capitalization, Merrill Lynch.

- Financial systems mobilize savings better by offering savers a range of savings vehicles.
- Financial systems allocate savings better by using expertise individual savers do not possess to ascertain potential borrower creditworthiness.
- Financial systems facilitate risk reduction to individual savers by diversifying pooled assets across many investment opportunities.

international comparisons of banking, see Brown and Skully (2003). These works and others point to a very limited pre-1990s literature on the subject, most particularly Goldsmith (1969) and McKinnon (1973). King and Levine (1993a and 1993b), Beck, Levine, and Loayza (2000), and others point to Joseph Schumpeter's insights in the early twentieth century as the intellectual antecedent to the recent literature on finance and growth.

- Financial systems augment liquidity by allowing savers to readily access savings while at the same time financial intermediaries fund long-term projects.
- Financial intermediaries contribute to better risk management by monitoring borrowers and managers of enterprises to which credit has been extended.

Researchers using cross-country data have begun to build a compelling case that financial sector development promotes economic growth, and much of this work focuses on the banking system.[3] For example, King and Levine (1993a), using data for 80 countries for 1960-1989, find a significantly positive relationship between several measures of financial development, including total credit extended to the private sector by banks, and economic growth. Their finding that the initial level of financial development in 1960 was a significant predictor of the subsequent average rate of growth over the next 29 years suggests a causal relationship between financial sector development and overall economic development.[4] More recently, Levine, Loayza and Beck (2000), using data for 74 countries, find that the exogenous component of financial intermediation is positively associated with economic growth. Also addressing the issue of causation, Rajan and Zingales (1998) used industry-level data for 41 countries in finding that industries more dependent on external financing tend to grow faster in countries with a higher level of financial system development, in which external financing – including credit extended by the banking sector – is easier to obtain. In a related vein, Demirgüç-Kunt and Maksimovic (2002) also use firm-level data across 40 countries to find that in more financially developed economies, a larger proportion of firms grew above the maximum rate of growth achievable by similar firms when they lacked access to external finance.

Yet even though a country's financial system is largely an intangible asset that can facilitate economic growth, it may fail to do so without an appropriate

[3] The focus on the banking system is due to the fact that all countries have banks and data on them are more readily available than for the capital markets. Indeed, underdeveloped bond markets in many countries and the unavailability of data has precluded any rigorous empirical research in this area as compared to banks and stock markets.

[4] For a critique of early-1990s studies on finance and growth, see Arestis and Demestriades (1997), which focuses on a number of thorny methodological difficulties to be overcome in order to establish causality between financial development and economic development. Note, nevertheless, that as Bonin and Wachtel (2003, p.1) observe, "A strong consensus has emerged in the last decade that well-functioning financial intermediaries have a significant impact on economic growth." Several single-country studies explore this issue. See, e.g., Bae, Kang, and Lim (2002) using Korean data; Ongena, Smith, and Michalsen (2003) using Norwegian data; and Gan (2003a) using Japanese data.

legal, regulatory, enforcement, and accounting environment.[5] The reason is that neither banks nor capital markets will function effectively in such situations; and without effective financial systems, weak economies will be unable to improve upon their relative position in the global economy.

THE ROLE OF BANKS

Recent literature on banking has emphasized the role banks play in reducing transaction costs, acting as delegated monitors for investors, and providing liquidity. It is these roles that distinguish banks from other financial institutions, and thus make bank regulation and supervision necessary.

Banks reduce transaction costs in the services they provide. Bank services can be viewed as transforming particular types of assets into others. Such transformation has two aspects. First, banks transform deposits with few or no restrictions on the minimal amount and of short-term maturity, such as demand deposits, into loans with a longer maturity and in larger amounts, and with credit risk. Thus they can be viewed as providing services of divisibility, maturity, and risk transformation. Second, banks provide payment services through the payment system.

These services are too costly for many individual economic actors to perform for themselves. For example, it would be costly for most investors to write debt contracts with firms directly because these are complex agreements with restrictive clauses on firm activities. Moreover, investors typically like to diversify their risks, which would multiply contracts and transaction costs. A bank is able to exploit returns to scale by writing and enforcing debt contract with firms. In the case of payment services, a firm or individual who receives a check does not have to verify the solvency of its issuer. Such verification for each transaction would be very costly. Centralizing this process at the level of financial intermediaries avoids wasteful duplication of verification costs.

The second role of banks lies in their ability to bridge information asymmetries in the credit markets by providing delegated monitoring (see, e.g., Diamond, 1984). There is a sizable literature on how banks may improve efficiency by reducing agency costs. A bank first screens potential borrowers either based on collateral or loan size (Bester, 1985; and Freixas and Laffont, 1990). Later, by auditing or, in the extreme, threatening to cut off credit, a bank

[5] In this regard, see La Porta, Lopez-de-Silanes, Shleifer, and Vishny (1998), Levine (1998) and Barth, Caprio and Levine (forthcoming).

prevents opportunistic behavior by the borrower (see, e.g., Stiglitz and Weiss, 1983; Diamond, 1984; and Holmstrom and Tirole, 1997). As a result, the bank is in a position to provide cheap "informed" funds as opposed to costly "uninformed" or arm's length funds (Fama, 1985; and James, 1987). Finally, there is a positive externality of bank monitoring in that other fixed-payoff claims need not undertake a similar costly evaluation (Easterbrook, 1984; and Besanko and Kanatas, 1993). Several studies have outlined possible negative consequences of banks' monitoring role. For example, Sharpe (1990) and Rajan (1992) study bank-borrower relationships in dynamic models in which banks try to establish "customer relationships" with borrowers in order to gather information about them. As information is only known to the bank, successful firms are locked into the relationship because they face switching costs if they decide to change their lenders. This results in monopoly rents for banks, and reduce incentives for firms to achieve higher profits.

While delegated monitoring concerns bank assets, the third role of banks, liquidity provision, is related to bank liabilities. In the famous Diamond and Dybvig (1983 and 2000) model, banks can be considered as a "pool of liquidity" that provides households with insurance against idiosyncratic shocks that affect their consumption needs. As long as these shocks are not perfectly correlated, by the law of large numbers, a large coalition of investors will be able to invest in illiquid but more profitable securities, while preserving enough liquidity to satisfy the needs of individual investors. However, this is also the source of a potential fragility of banks. In the event that a high number of depositors decide to withdraw, banks have to liquidate long-term investments and incur economic losses. They then face the risk of not being able to repay depositors who withdraw later. Therefore, if a significant number of depositors have withdrawn, other depositors would imitate them, resulting in bank runs. Banks face the following dilemma: either they invest in short-term assets and do not fulfill their asset transformation role, which is inefficient; or they efficiently fulfill their asset transformation role but they face the possibility of bank runs when they invest at least partially in illiquid long-term assets. How to ensure a banking system obtains a proper balance between efficiency and stability is a central issue in bank regulation and supervision.

A combination of the above three roles distinguish banks from other financial institutions and suggest that bank loans are unique and special. Empirically, there is some evidence supporting the uniqueness of bank loans. Earlier literature looks at stock price responses to announcements of bank loans and other types of debt, such as private placements and public debt issues. James (1987) finds that there is a positive stock price response to a borrower's acquisition of bank loans but a negative response to debt placed privately with insurance companies. Recent literature further examines the causes of such uniqueness by looking at the relationship between bank health and firm performance (e.g., Slovin, Sushka and Poloncheck, 1993; Gibson, 1995; Kang and Stulz, 2000; Bae, Kang, and Lim, 2002; Peek and Rosengren, 2000; Ongena, Smith, and Michalsen, 2003; and Gan, 2003b). Most of these studies find evidence that banking relationships are valuable insofar as negative shocks to bank health are associated with lower stock market valuations and/or lower fixed investments.

The value of durable banking relationships also suggests a "credit channel" as a transmission mechanism of monetary policy. Bernanke and Blinder (1992), Kashyap, Stein, and Wilcox (1993), and Hoshi, Sharfstein, and Singleton (1993) present evidence that bank loan volume decreases during monetary contractions, and the latter two papers further document a rise in commercial paper issuance. A more direct test of bank credit constraints is by Kashyap and Stein (2000), who demonstrate, using aggregate bank-level loan data, that more liquid banks are less likely to reduce lending during monetary contractions than less liquid banks.

THE RELATIVE IMPORTANCE OF BANKS IN THE WORLD FINANCIAL SYSTEM

The relative role of stocks, bonds, and bank loans in providing external funding for firms has been changing over time. As can be seen in Figures 1 and 2, the banking share of the world financial system has declined to 37 percent in 2001 from 49 percent in 1990. This relative decline largely reflects the fact that mature economies simply do not need the same size banking system as they did during their more formative growth years. Even in Germany, with a bank-based financial system, moreover, the relative importance of banks has declined 6 percentage points over the past decade (see Figure 3). And in the U.S., with a capital markets-based financial system, the banking share of the financial system declined 8 percentage points over the same time period, as illustrated in Figure 3.

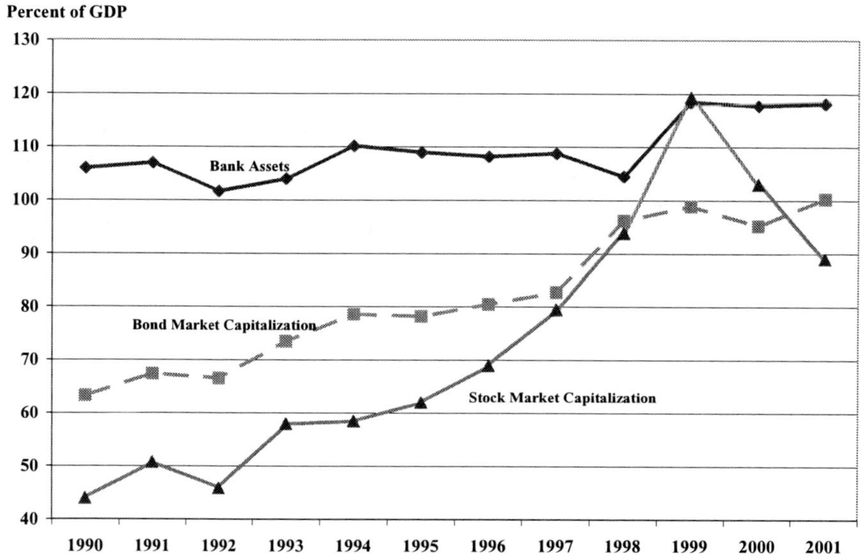

Source: International Financial Statistics, International Monetary Fund; Size of World Bond Market Capitalization, Merrill Lynch and Emerging Stock Market Factbook, Standard & Poor's.

Figure 1. Changing Structure of World Financial System.

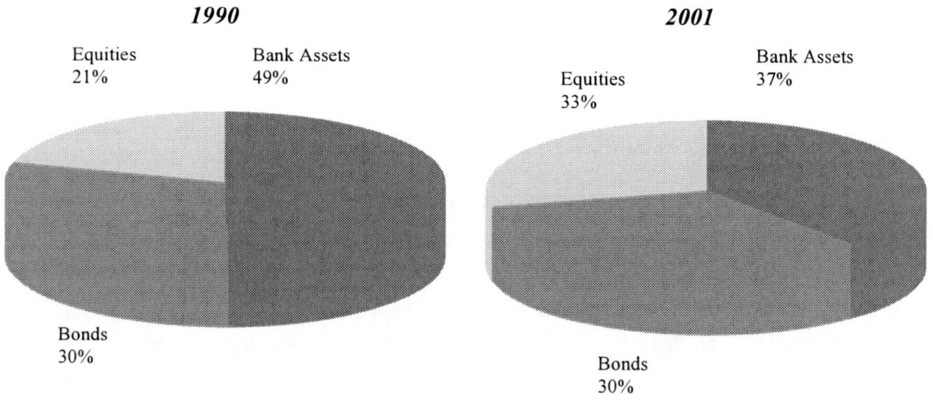

Figure 2. Banking Share of World Financial System Diminishes.

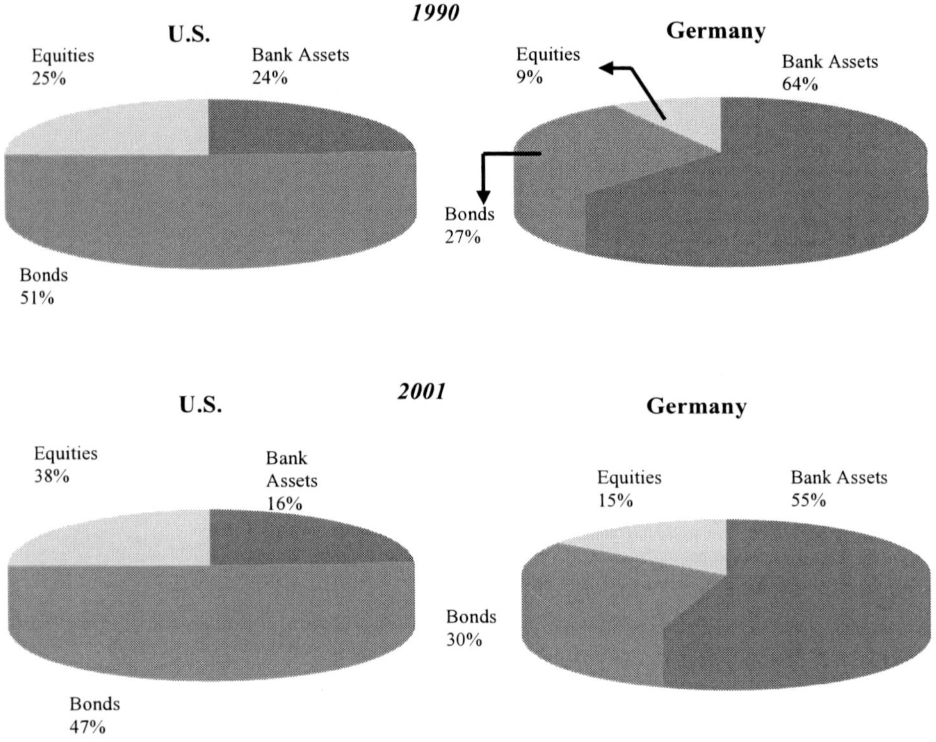

Source: International Financial Statistics, International Monetary Fund; Size of World Bond Market Capitalization, Merrill Lynch and Emerging Stock Market Factbook, Standard & Poor'

Figure 3. Bank-Based vs. Market-Based Financial Systems.

There is still some disagreement among economists about whether a bank-based or capital markets-based financial system contributes most to the overall development of an economy.[6] It does appear, however, that a consensus is emerging that banks (or loans) and capital markets (or securities) are complements, not substitutes, in promoting economic development. This means that both play important, albeit different, roles in channeling funds from savers to investors.[7] Bank financing, however, tends to dominate in developing countries. But capital markets become more important than banks as countries mature and

[6] See Allen and Gale (2000).

[7] See Demirgüç-Kunt and Levine (2001).

evolve into service-oriented economies.[8] Nonetheless, policy actions should not be taken that favor one source of external financing by firms over the other.[9]

Table 2. Structure of Banking Systems: International Comparisons

Country	Bank Assets/GDP (%)	% of Bank Assets in Top 5 Banks	Noninterest Revenue/Total Revenue (%)	Fraction of Capital in the Largest 10 Banks Owned by Commercial/Industrial and/or Financial Conglomerates
High Income				
Australia	116	76	41	<10%
Belgium	408	88	44	90
Canada	150	80	52	0
Cyprus	246	89	54	n.a.
Denmark	146	90	39	n.a.
Finland	83	100	20	94
France	n.a.	60	85	n.a.
Germany	305	20	n.a.	n.a.
Greece	133	74	24	0
Hong Kong, China	467	42	13	n.a.
Israel	147	93	35	<5%
Italy	154	51	45	0
Japan	167	46	38	n.a.
Korea	101	70	28	0
Kuwait	110	88	14	n.a.
Luxembourg	3,427	28	49	0
Netherlands	408	88	43	n.a.

[8] The growth of electronic finance may add a substantial dimension to the finance-and-growth dynamic, as discussed in Claessens, Glaessner, and Klingebiel (2001, and 2002). In particular, they point to evidence suggesting that developing countries may be able to "leapfrog" past the development of some components of traditional financial services infrastructure by adopting online and remote delivery mechanisms for financial services. Both studies included detailed cross-country comparisons of e-finance. Though still at relatively modest levels in most countries, growth in some electronic delivery channels is significant across countries at different stages of economic development.

[9] Barth, Caudill, Hall and Yago (2000) find some evidence that the costs of banking crisis are higher in countries in which the financial system is more heavily dependent upon banks.

Table 2. Continued

Country	Bank Assets/GDP (%)	% of Bank Assets in Top 5 Banks	Noninterest Revenue/Total Revenue (%)	Fraction of Capital in the Largest 10 Banks Owned by Commercial/Industrial and/or Financial Conglomerates
New Zealand	156	86	36	n.a.
Norway	49	84	14	n.a.
Portugal	217	80	54	99
Singapore	1,200	n.a.	n.a.	n.a.
Slovenia	82	69	4	8 of 10 banks owned by financial conglomerates
Spain	186	53	27	0
Sweden	127	n.a.	54	A non-significant fraction
Switzerland	537	72	40	n.a.
United Kingdom	352	23	40	100
United States	65	27	28	37
Average	*206**	*67*	*37*	*38*
Upper Middle Income				
Argentina	45	50	31	n.a.
Botswana	31	100	21	0
Chile	102	61	42	88
Czech Republic	135	69	3	93
Estonia	70	99	34	n.a.
Hungary	66	63	n.a.	62
Lithuania	32	88	28	n.a.
Malaysia	202	56	15	50
Mauritius	93	91	16	4
Mexico	28	80	19	n.a.
Oman	55	86	22	12
Panama	374	14	13	57
Poland	64	57	n.a.	0
Saudi Arabia	67	73	12	n.a.
Slovakia	94	67	n.a.	93
Uruguay	110	50	4	7 of 10 banks owned by financial conglomerates
Venezuela	5	57	n.a.	n.a.
Average	*92*	*68*	*20*	*46*
Lower Middle Income				

Bolivia	58	71	42	39
Brazil	78	54	0	n.a.
China	197	72	8	n.a.
Colombia	36	41	n.a.	n.a.
Ecuador	27	70	2	100
Egypt	100	62	n.a.	0
El Salvador	65	87	12	n.a.
Guatemala	34	55	90	n.a.
Jordan	216	62	10	n.a.
Morocco	87	66	9	8
Peru	34	83	24	89
Philippines	80	43	17	n.a.
Romania	28	65	50	N/A
Russia	34	43	74	n.a.
South Africa	76	75	56	n.a.
Thailand	126	65	14	65
Turkey	75	56	9	27
Average	*80*	*63*	*28*	*47*
Low Income				
Azerbaijan	14	72	n.a.	0
Ghana	37	78	37	n.a.
India	62	44	13	7
Kenya	45	60	23	40
Kyrgyzstan	7	51	n.a.	0
Moldova	41	71	39	n.a.
Nicaragua	72	92	11	n.a.
Niger	11	97	n.a.	n.a.
Nigeria	43	41	36	30
Pakistan	51	65	n.a.	n.a.
Rwanda	17	96	76	n.a.
Zimbabwe	61	68	n.a.	52.3
Average	*39*	*69*	*33*	*21*

Source: Office of the Comptroller of the Currency and World Bank using information from national supervisory authorities and People's Bank of China Annual Report

Notes:

* average excludes Cyprus, Luxembourg and Singapore.

n.a. and N/A signify, respectively, not available, not applicable.

The income groups are based on the World Bank country classification of economies as of July 2003. The economies are grouped according to 2002 gross national income (GNI) per capita. The groups are defined as follows: low income, $735 or less; lower middle income,$736–2,935; upper middle income, $2,936–9,075; and high income, $9,075 or more.

Even though the relative importance of banks has declined, they nevertheless remain quite important. This fact is reflected in the information in Table 2. As may be seen, in the high-income countries the average ratio of bank assets-to-GDP is 206 percent. And these are the countries that typically have broad, deep, and liquid securities markets. The percentages decline as one moves from this group of countries to the low-income group of countries, which has an average bank assets-to-GDP ratio of 39 percent. The lower-income groups of countries therefore have relatively underdeveloped banking systems even though firms are typically heavily dependent upon banks for external finance.

There are, however, some notable deviations in the bank assets-to-GDP ratios among the high-income countries. The U.S., for example, has a bank assets-to-GDP ratio of only 65 percent. Taking into account not only the banking system, but also stocks and bonds, the U.S. has the largest financial system of the world. Hence, its relatively small bank assets-to-GDP ratio is not a reflection of an underdeveloped banking system, but rather an indication of the relatively lower level importance of the banking system compared with the stock and bond markets.[10]

The declining relative importance of banks, despite their still absolute importance, has increased competitive pressures on them to consolidate and to expand the range of services they offer. These developments are reflected in Table 2. The average concentration ratio of bank assets among the five largest banks for the low-income countries is 69 percent. While such a high ratio might not seem unusual for such countries that frequently have relatively few banks, the comparable ratio for the high-income countries is nearly the same at 67 percent. The ratio for the other two categories of countries, moreover, differs from this by no more than 6 percentage points. Such a high ratio reflects the trend towards greater consolidation in the banking sectors across countries.

The trend for banks to move from relying almost exclusively on net interest income to depending more significantly on non-interest revenue as a source of profits is also reflected in Table 2. Regardless of income level, banks in countries around the world on average receive between about 20 to 37 percent of their total revenue from non-interest sources.[11] The higher percentage, however, is for the high-income countries.

The declining importance of banks as compared to capital markets, moreover, is overstated to the extent that banks are part of a financial or non-financial conglomerate. Table 2 presents information showing that this is indeed the case in many countries regardless of income level. Indeed, the percentage of capital in the 10 largest banks owned by such conglomerates ranges from a low of 21 percent

---

[10] For a comprehensive analysis of how and why the composition of financial systems differs across countries, see Allen and Gale (2000).

[11] One possibility for a high non-interest revenue-to-total revenue ratio, particularly in less developed financial systems, in that a large proportion of non-interest revenue may be accounted for by deposit charges and similar fees which are directly tied to "traditional" interest-bearing services, and hence not reflective of product diversification.

for the low-income countries, to 47 percent for the lower-middle-income countries, to 46 percent for the higher-middle-income countries, and to 38 percent for the upper-income countries. These figures, and taking into account off-balance sheet activities, demonstrate that banks still play an important role in financial systems around the globe.

WHAT IS A BANK?

The banking industry is regulated and supervised in every country around the globe, but wide differences exist with respect to the activities in which banks are permitted to engage. Some countries restrict banks to a narrow range of activities, whereas others allow them to engage in a broad array. Since it is the scope of activities that essentially defines the term "bank," a bank is therefore not the same in every country around the world.[12] It is the regulatory authorities, moreover, who not only determine the extent to which the activities of banks differ across countries, but also the extent to which they differ from nonbank-financial and nonfinancial firms within countries.

Table 3 presents information on the differences in permissible activities for banks in countries grouped by income level. The activities include the ability of banks to engage in the business of securities underwriting, brokering, and dealing; insurance underwriting and selling; and real estate investment, development, and management. The degree to which these activities are restricted is denoted by the terms unrestricted, permitted, restricted and prohibited. These designations are based upon Barth, Caprio and Levine (2001b), with each country's regulations concerning each of these activities rated on the degree of restrictiveness from 1 to 4.[13] These numbers correspond to the four designations, unrestricted through

---

[12] For an interesting discussion of the evolution of the legal definition of a bank in the U.S., see Haubrich and Santos (2003, pp.147-148). In a similar vein, there is the issue as to what is meant by the term "banking product." To a growing extent product convergence is occurring, in which similar financial products are offered by different financial service industries. The regulatory and supervisory issue is that those products may in effect receive different regulatory treatment because they are being offered from differently regulated industries. For example, there is a growing similarity between performance standby letters of credit typically issued by banks, and surety bonds typically issued by insurance firms.

[13] More specifically, unrestricted means a full range of activities can be conducted in the bank; permitted means a full range of activities can be conducted, but some or all must be conducted in subsidiaries; restricted means less than a full range of activities can be conducted in the bank or subsidiaries; prohibited means the activity cannot be conducted in either the bank or subsidiaries. For bank ownership of nonfinancial firms: unrestricted means a bank may own 100 percent of the equity in any nonfinancial firm; permitted means a bank may own 100 percent of

prohibited, with the higher number indicating greater restrictiveness. This approach enables one to construct an index of activities restrictiveness that ranges in value from 3 (least restrictive) to 12 (most restrictive).

Table 3 shows that securities activities are the least restricted and real estate activities are the most restricted in countries across all income levels. Indeed, only two of the 73 countries prohibit banks from engaging in securities activities. In contrast, slightly more than one-third of the countries prohibit them from engaging in real estate activities. Nicaragua is the only country that prohibits banks from engaging in securities, insurance, and real estate activities. Panama and Oman are interesting because they prohibit insurance and real estate activities for banks yet allow them unrestricted securities activities. At the other end of the restrictiveness spectrum, four countries grant banks unrestricted securities, insurance, and real estate powers – Estonia, Germany, New Zealand, and Switzerland. Recently, a few countries have become more liberal in granting banks broader powers. The U.S., for example, with the enactment of the Gramm-Leach-Bliley Act (GLBA) in late 1999, now permits rather than restricts banks' access to both securities and insurance activities.[14]

The degree of restrictiveness on the mixing of banking and commerce, or the creation of financial conglomerates, also displays substantial variation across countries (see Table 4). Banks' ownership of nonfinancial firms is more restricted than nonfinancial firm ownership of banks. About 10 percent of the countries prohibit bank ownership of nonfinancial firms, whereas only one country prohibits ownership of banks by nonfinancial firms. Only the U.S. prohibits the mixing of banking and commerce.[15] It is also important to note that only Kenya prohibits nonbank financial firms from owning banks. Based on the index of overall restrictiveness, the least restrictive countries are New Zealand, the United Kingdom, and Brazil; El Salvador, Nicaragua, and the U.S. are tied for being the

the equity in a nonfinancial firm, but ownership is limited based on a bank's equity capital; restricted means a bank can only acquire less than 100 percent of the equity in a nonfinancial firm; prohibited means a bank may not acquire any equity investment in a nonfinancial firm. For nonfinancial firm ownership of banks: unrestricted means a nonfinancial firm may own 100 percent of the equity in a bank; permitted means unrestricted, but need prior authorization or approval; restricted means limits are placed on ownership, such as a maximum percentage of a bank's capital or shares; prohibited means no equity investment in a bank is allowed.

14 See Barth, Brumbaugh, and Wilcox (2000). As a result of GLBA, however, the U.S. in some respects has tightened restrictions on the mixing of banking and commerce.

15 Note that the World Bank survey asks for responses at the bank level. The U.S. allows bank holding companies and financial holding companies to own both bank and nonbank firms, subject to certain restrictions. See Barth, Brumbaugh, and Wilcox (2000) for a basic discussion of these possibilities under the Gramm-Leach-Bliley Act of 1999.

most restrictive. More generally, there is a tendency for high-income countries to be less restrictive than countries in the three other income groups.

Table 3. What is a Bank? Permissible Banking Activities: International Comparisons (Countries ranked from least to most restrictive)

Country	Securities	Insurance	Real Estate	Index of Activities Restrictiveness (a higher number indicates greater restrictiveness)
High Income				
Germany	Unrestricted	Unrestricted	Unrestricted	3
Luxembourg	Unrestricted	Unrestricted	Unrestricted	3
New Zealand	Unrestricted	Unrestricted	Unrestricted	3
France	Unrestricted	Permitted	Unrestricted	4
Spain	Unrestricted	Permitted	Unrestricted	4
United Kingdom	Unrestricted	Permitted	Unrestricted	4
Hong Kong, China	Unrestricted	Permitted	Unrestricted	4
Denmark	Permitted	Permitted	Unrestricted	5
Netherlands	Unrestricted	Restricted	Unrestricted	5
Portugal	Unrestricted	Unrestricted	Restricted	5
Switzerland	Unrestricted	Restricted	Unrestricted	5
Kuwait	Unrestricted	Permitted	Permitted	5
Norway	Permitted	Permitted	Unrestricted	5
Cyprus	Unrestricted	Unrestricted	Prohibited	6
Finland	Permitted	Permitted	Permitted	6
Italy	Unrestricted	Unrestricted	Prohibited	6
Belgium	Unrestricted	Restricted	Restricted	7
Canada	Restricted	Restricted	Unrestricted	7
Singapore	Unrestricted	Restricted	Restricted	7
Sweden	Permitted	Permitted	Restricted	7
Australia	Permitted	Permitted	Prohibited	8
Greece	Permitted	Restricted	Restricted	8
Japan	Permitted	Permitted	Prohibited	8
Korea	Permitted	Permitted	Prohibited	8
United States	Permitted	Permitted	Prohibited	8
Slovenia	Restricted	Restricted	Restricted	9
Israel	Permitted	Prohibited	Prohibited	10

Table 3. Continued

Country	Securities	Insurance	Real Estate	Index of Activities Restrictiveness (a higher number indicates greater restrictiveness)
Average				*5.93*
Upper Middle Income				
Estonia	Unrestricted	Unrestricted	Unrestricted	3
Argentina	Permitted	Unrestricted	Restricted	6
Lithuania	Permitted	Permitted	Permitted	6
Mexico	Permitted	Permitted	Permitted	6
Poland	Permitted	Permitted	Permitted	6
Saudi Arabia	Unrestricted	Unrestricted	Prohibited	6
Venezuela	Permitted	Permitted	Permitted	6
Slovakia	Unrestricted	Unrestricted	Prohibited	6
Uruguay	Unrestricted	Unrestricted	Prohibited	6
Botswana	Permitted	Unrestricted	Prohibited	7
Malaysia	Restricted	Unrestricted	Restricted	7
Hungary	Permitted	Permitted	Restricted	7
Chile	Permitted	Permitted	Prohibited	8
Czech Republic	Permitted	Permitted	Prohibited	8
Panama	Unrestricted	Prohibited	Prohibited	9
Oman	Unrestricted	Prohibited	Prohibited	9
Mauritius	Restricted	Prohibited	Prohibited	11
Average				*6.88*
Lower Middle Income				
Peru	Permitted	Unrestricted	Permitted	5
Philippines	Unrestricted	Permitted	Permitted	5
Russia	Permitted	Permitted	Permitted	5
South Africa	Permitted	Unrestricted	Permitted	5
Guatemala	Permitted	Permitted	Permitted	6
Turkey	Permitted	Permitted	Permitted	6
Brazil	Unrestricted	Permitted	Prohibited	7
Jordan	Unrestricted	Permitted	Prohibited	7
Egypt	Restricted	Permitted	Restricted	8
Morocco	Permitted	Restricted	Restricted	8
Bolivia	Permitted	Restricted	Prohibited	9
Romania	Permitted	Restricted	Prohibited	9
Thailand	Restricted	Restricted	Restricted	9

China	Restricted	Restricted	Prohibited	10
Colombia	Permitted	Prohibited	Prohibited	10
Ecuador	Prohibited	Permitted	Prohibited	10
El Salvador	Restricted	Restricted	Prohibited	10
Average				*7.59*
Low Income				
Kenya	Permitted	Permitted	Permitted	6
Kyrgyzstan	Unrestricted	Prohibited	Unrestricted	6
Niger	Permitted	Permitted	Permitted	6
Rwanda	Unrestricted	Unrestricted	Prohibited	6
Zimbabwe	Permitted	Permitted	Restricted	7
Azerbaijan	Restricted	Prohibited	Unrestricted	8
Ghana	Permitted	Prohibited	Permitted	8
India	Permitted	Permitted	Prohibited	8
Pakistan	Permitted	Permitted	Prohibited	8
Nigeria	Restricted	Restricted	Restricted	9
Moldova	Restricted	Prohibited	Prohibited	11
Nicaragua	Prohibited	Prohibited	Prohibited	12
Average				*7.92*

Source: World Bank Regulation and Supervision Survey (2003); and *Global Survey 2003*, Institute of International Bankers.

Notes:

Securities: the ability of banks to engage in the business of securities underwriting, brokering, dealing, and all aspects of the mutual funds industry.

Insurance: the ability of banks to engage in insurance underwriting and selling.

Real Estate: the ability of banks to engage in real estate investment, development, and management.

Activities

Unrestricted = a full range of activities can be conducted in the bank. Takes an index value of 1.

Permitted = a full range of activities can be conducted, but some or all must be conducted in subsidiaries. Takes an index value of 2.

Restricted = less than a full range of activities can be conducted in the bank or subsidiaries. Takes an index value of 3.

Prohibited = the activity cannot be conducted in either the bank or subsidiaries. Takes an index value of 4.

Differences among countries in the regulatory treatment of permissible activities for banks and the formation of financial conglomerates are wide, but all countries share the ultimate regulatory and supervisory goal of promoting systemic stability. Additionally, regulation and supervision may also be aimed at promoting the development and efficiency of the banking sector. The important issue is what mix of permissible activities and degree of financial conglomeration is best for banks in each country around the world to achieve these goals.

Table 4. Financial Conglomeration: International Comparisons (Countries ranked from least to most restrictive)

Country	Bank Ownership of Nonfinancial Firms	Nonfinancial Firm Ownership of Banks	Non-Bank Financial Firm Ownership of Banks	Overall Restrictiveness (a higher number indicates greater restrictiveness)
High Income				
New Zealand	Unrestricted	Unrestricted	Unrestricted	3
United Kingdom	Unrestricted	Unrestricted	Unrestricted	3
Greece	Permitted	Unrestricted	Unrestricted	4
Switzerland	Permitted	Unrestricted	Unrestricted	4
Spain	Unrestricted	Permitted	Permitted	5
Sweden	Unrestricted	Permitted	Permitted	5
Kuwait	Permitted	Permitted	Unrestricted	5
Australia	Permitted	Permitted	Permitted	6
Belgium	Permitted	Permitted	Permitted	6
Finland	Permitted	Permitted	Permitted	6
France	Permitted	Permitted	Permitted	6
Germany	Permitted	Permitted	Permitted	6
Netherlands	Permitted	Permitted	Permitted	6
Denmark	Restricted	Permitted	Permitted	7
Hong Kong, China	Permitted	Restricted	Permitted	7
Japan	Restricted	Permitted	Permitted	7
Korea	Restricted	Permitted	Permitted	7
Luxembourg	Restricted	Permitted	Permitted	7
Norway	Permitted	Restricted	Permitted	7
Portugal	Restricted	Permitted	Permitted	7
Singapore	Restricted	Permitted	Permitted	7
Slovenia	Restricted	Permitted	Permitted	7
Canada	Permitted	Restricted	Restricted	8
Italy	Restricted	Restricted	Permitted	8
Cyprus	Restricted	Restricted	Restricted	9
Israel	Restricted	Restricted	Restricted	9
United States	Prohibited	Prohibited	Permitted	10
Average				*6.37*
Upper Middle Income				
Poland	Unrestricted	Permitted	Unrestricted	4
Botswana	Permitted	Unrestricted	Permitted	5

Country	Bank Ownership of Nonfinancial Firms	Nonfinancial Firm Ownership of Banks	Non-Bank Financial Firm Ownership of Banks	Overall Restrictiveness (a higher number indicates greater restrictiveness)
Estonia	Permitted	Permitted	Permitted	6
Lithuania	Permitted	Permitted	Permitted	6
Panama	Permitted	Permitted	Permitted	6
Saudi Arabia	Restricted	Unrestricted	Permitted	6
Argentina	Restricted	Permitted	Permitted	7
Czech Republic	Restricted	Permitted	Permitted	7
Hungary	Restricted	Permitted	Permitted	7
Slovakia	Restricted	Permitted	Permitted	7
Venezuela	Restricted	Permitted	Permitted	7
Chile	Prohibited	Permitted	Permitted	8
Mauritius	Permitted	Restricted	Restricted	8
Uruguay	Prohibited	Permitted	Permitted	8
Malaysia	Restricted	Restricted	Restricted	9
Mexico	Restricted	Restricted	Restricted	9
Oman	Restricted	Restricted	Restricted	9
Average				*7.00*
Lower Middle Income				
Brazil	Unrestricted	Unrestricted	Unrestricted	3
South Africa	Permitted	Permitted	Unrestricted	5
Bolivia	Prohibited	Unrestricted	Unrestricted	6
Guatemala	Permitted	Permitted	Permitted	6
Peru	Permitted	Permitted	Permitted	6
Turkey	Permitted	Permitted	Permitted	6
Russia	Permitted	Permitted	Permitted	6
Jordan	Restricted	Permitted	Permitted	7
Morocco	Restricted	Permitted	Permitted	7
Romania	Restricted	Permitted	Permitted	7
Thailand	Permitted	Restricted	Permitted	7
Colombia	Restricted	Permitted	Permitted	7
Egypt	Restricted	Permitted	Permitted	7
China	Prohibited	Permitted	Permitted	8
Ecuador	Prohibited	Permitted	Permitted	8
Philippines	Permitted	Restricted	Restricted	8
El Salvador	Prohibited	Restricted	Restricted	10
Average				*6.71*
Low Income				

Country	Bank Ownership of Nonfinancial Firms	Nonfinancial Firm Ownership of Banks	Non-Bank Financial Firm Ownership of Banks	Overall Restrictiveness (a higher number indicates greater restrictiveness)
Moldova	Permitted	Permitted	Permitted	6
Azerbaijan	Permitted	Restricted	Unrestricted	6
Ghana	Permitted	Permitted	Permitted	6
Niger	Restricted	Permitted	Permitted	7
Nigeria	Restricted	Permitted	Permitted	7
Pakistan	Restricted	Permitted	Permitted	7
Rwanda	Restricted	Permitted	Permitted	7
Kenya	Unrestricted	Restricted	Prohibited	8
Kyrgyzstan	Permitted	Restricted	Restricted	8
India	Restricted	Restricted	Restricted	9
Zimbabwe	Restricted	Restricted	Restricted	9
Nicaragua	Prohibited	Restricted	Restricted	10
Average				*7.50*

Source: World Bank Regulation and Supervision Survey (2003); and *Global Survey 2003*, Institute of International Bankers.

Notes:

Bank ownership of Nonfinancial firms

Unrestricted = A bank may own 100 percent of the equity in any nonfinancial firm.

Permitted = A bank may own 100 percent of the equity in a nonfinancial firm, but ownership is limited based on a bank's equity capital.

Restricted = A bank can only acquire less than 100 percent of the equity in a nonfinancial firm.

Prohibited = A bank may not acquire any equity investment in a nonfinancial firm.

Nonfinancial firm ownership of banks

Unrestricted = A Nonfinancial firm may own 100 percent of the equity in a bank.

Permitted = Unrestricted, but need prior authorization or approval.

Restricted = Limits are placed on ownership, such as a maximum percentage of a bank's capital or shares.

Prohibited = No equity investment in a bank is allowed.

Non-bank financial firm ownership of banks

Unrestriced = Non-bank financial firms may own 100% of the equity in a commercial bank

Permitted = Non-bank financial firms may own 100% of the equity in a commercial bank; but prior authorization or approval is required

Restricted = Limits are placed on ownership of banks by nonfinancial firms, such as maximum percentage of a commercial bank's capital or shares

Prohibited = Non-bank financial firms cannot own any equity investment in a commercial bank whatsoever

At the theoretical level, there are arguments on both sides of the issue. The main reasons for restricting the permissible activities of banks and the creation of financial conglomerates are as follows:

- Conflicts of interest may arise when banks are allowed to engage in a diverse group of activities, either separately or as part of a financial conglomerate.[16]
- Banks will have more opportunities to increase risk when allowed to engage in a broader range of activities, which they are more likely to do when they have access to deposit insurance, either separately or as a part of a financial conglomerate.[17]
- The wider the range of activities, the greater the likelihood that the activities will be done through the formation of financial conglomerates that may be extraordinarily difficult to supervise.[18]
- Large institutions or financial conglomerates may become so politically and economically powerful that they become "too big to discipline."
- Lastly, the creation of financial conglomerates may reduce competition and thus efficiency in the entire financial sector.

There are theoretical reasons, however, for allowing banks to engage in a broad range of activities, perhaps especially through the establishment of financial conglomerates. Fewer regulatory restrictions on the activities of banks may:

- Permit the exploitation of economies of scale and scope in gathering and processing information about firms, managing different types of risk for customers, advertising and distributing financial services, enforcing contracts, and building reputational capital with clients.
- Increase the franchise value of banks and thereby enhance their incentive to behave prudently.
- Lead to diversified income streams and thus create more stable banks.
- Limit the ability of the government to use banks to allocate funds to less productive projects, and thereby promote bank performance and stability.[19]

---

[16] See, e.g., Edwards (1979) and John, John and Saunders (1994).
[17] See, e.g., Boyd, Change and Smith (1998).
[18] Michael Camdessus (1997), e.g., remarked that we are witnessing "...the organization of financial conglomerates, whose scope is often hard to grasp and whose operations may be impossible for outside observers -- even bank supervisors -- to monitor."
[19] Saunders (1994) provides a good review that focuses specifically on the potential benefits and costs of mixing banking and commerce.

Although existing empirical studies do not fully resolve these theoretical debates, most of the literature suggests there are positive benefits from permitting banks broad powers. Most recently, Barth, Caprio, and Levine (forthcoming), in an analysis of the largest group of countries to date, find that restricting bank activities is negatively associated with bank performance and stability, as compared to when banks can diversify into other financial activities. These results are consistent with the view that broad banking powers allow banks to diversify income sources and enhance stability. Their finding, moreover, is not due to reverse causality.[20] Furthermore, extending their earlier study, they control for official supervisory practices, capital regulations, regulations on competition, government ownership of banks, and the moral hazard engendered by generous deposit insurance schemes. The negative relationship between restricting bank activities and bank development and stability therefore does not seem to be because of an obvious omitted variable. Furthermore, they find no evidence that restricting bank activities produces positive results in particular institutional or policy environments. Specifically, they do not find improvements in bank performance or stability from restrictions on bank activities in economies that offer more generous deposit insurance, have weak official supervision, ineffective incentives for private monitoring, or that lack stringent capital standards.[21]

[20] See Barth, Caprio, and Levine (2001a) for a discussion of this issue.

[21] For a more through review of the literature in this area, see Barth, Caprio and Nolle (forthcoming).

Chapter 2

Regulation and Supervision of Banks

Who Supervises Banks?

Banking crises, rapid structural change, and the continuing globalization of banking have led national and multilateral policy makers to focus increased attention on the crucial role of banking supervision. This focus is reinforced by the fact that "…one of the important [international] trends has been, and continues to be, a move away from regulation and towards supervision."[22] Policy discussions specifically focus on several issues that must be addressed in establishing and maintaining effective supervision, including who should supervise banks, i.e., the "structure" of bank supervision. Three issues for policy makers to address with respect to the structure of bank supervision are whether there should be a single bank supervisory authority, or multiple bank supervisors; whether the central bank should play a role in bank supervision; and whether the supervisor responsible for the banking industry should also have responsibility for other financial services, in particular the securities and insurance industries. How these issues are addressed is important because policies that fail to provide for an appropriate bank supervisory framework may undermine bank performance and even lead to full-scale banking crises.

---

[22]Crockett (2001).

Single Bank Supervisor or Multiple Bank Supervisors

A key policy decision in designing the structure of the bank supervisory system is whether there should be a single bank supervisory authority or multiple bank supervisors. Although previous conceptual literature covers a number of possible advantages and disadvantages to each option, perhaps the strongest reason for some to advocate a single bank supervisory authority is the fear of a "competition in laxity" between multiple bank supervisors, while those who favor a system with two or more bank supervisors stress the benefits of a "competition in ideas" among multiple bank supervisors.[23]

One essential set of information largely missing from the previous literature on the issue of the structure of bank supervision is what different countries around the world have chosen to do. Table 5 provides information on the international "landscape" of bank supervisory structure. The vast majority of countries have a single bank supervisory authority. Nevertheless, 5 percent of the 73 countries, including the U.S., assign banking supervision to multiple supervisory authorities.[24]

Table 5. The Structure of Bank Supervision: International Comparisons

Country	Bank Supervisory Authority	Single Bank Supervisor or Multiple Bank Supervisors	Role of Central Bank[1]
High Income			
Australia[2]	Australian Prudential Regulation Authority (APRA)	Single	NCB
Belgium	Commission for Banking and Finance (CBF)	Single	NCB
Canada	Office of the Superintendent of Financial Institutions (OSFI)	Single	NCB
Cyprus	Central Bank of Cyprus	Single	CB
Denmark	Danish Financial Supervisory	Single	NCB

[23] See Barth, Nolle, Phumiwasana, and Yago (2003, pp. 70-73) for a detailed discussion of the advantages and disadvantages of single supervisor and multiple supervisors systems of bank regulation. Also, see Barth, Dopico, Nolle and Wilcox (2002).

[24] Briault (1999, pp.15-16) briefly discusses the issue of a transnational financial services supervisor. See also the discussion in the Biship (2002). Transnational issues also come into play in the debate over financial supervision in the European Union. See, e.g., Lannoo (2000), and International Monetary Fund (2001), Goodhart (2002), and Schüler (2003).

Country	Bank Supervisory Authority	Single Bank Supervisor or Multiple Bank Supervisors	Role of Central Bank[1]
	Authority (DFSA)		
Finland	Financial Supervision Authority	Single	NCB
France	Commission Bancaire	Single	NCB
Germany	Federal Financial Supervisory Authority (BaFin), Deutche Bundesbank	Multiple	CB
Greece	Bank of Greece	Single	CB
Hong Kong, China	Hong Kong Monetary Authority	Single	NCB
Israel	Bank of Israel	Single	CB
Italy	Bank of Italy	Single	CB
Japan	Financial Services Agency	Single	NCB
Korea	Financial Supervisory Commission	Single	NCB
Kuwait	Central Bank of Kuwait (CBK)	Single	CB
Luxembourg	Commission de Surveillance du Secteur Financier (CSSF)	Single	NCB
Netherlands	De Nederlandsche Bank	Single	CB
New Zealand	Reserve Bank of New Zealand	Single	CB
Norway	Banking Insurance and Securities Commission of Norway	Single	NCB
Portugal	Bank of Portugal	Single	CB
Singapore	Monetary Authority of Singapore	Single	CB
Slovenia	Bank of Slovenia	Single	CB
Spain	Bank of Spain	Single	CB
Sweden	Swedish Financial Supervisory Authority	Single	NCB
Switzerland	Swiss Federal Banking Commission (SFBC)	Single	NCB
United Kingdom	Financial Services Authority (FSA)	Single	NCB
United States[3]	Office of the Comptroller of the Currency, Federal Reserve System, Federal Deposit Insurance Corporation	Multiple	CB
Summary Characteristics for High Income Countries		*93% Single*	*48% CB*

Table 5. Continued

Upper Middle Income			
Argentina	Central Bank of Republic Argentina	Single	CB
Botswana	Central Bank of Botswana	Single	CB
Chile	Superintendency of Banks and Financial Institutions (SBIF)	Single	NCB
Czech Republic	Czech National Bank	Single	CB
Estonia	Estonian Financial Supervision Authority	Single	NCB
Hungary	Hungary Financial Supervisory Authority	Single	NCB
Lithuania	Bank of Lithuania	Single	CB
Malaysia	Bank Negara Malaysia	Single	CB
Mauritius	Bank of Mauritius	Single	CB
Mexico	National Banking and Securities Commission	Single	NCB
Oman	Central Bank of Oman	Single	CB
Panama	Superintendent of Banks	Single	NCB
Poland[4]	Commission for Banking Supervision of the National Bank of Poland	Single	CB
Saudi Arabia	Saudi Arabian Monetary Authority (SAMA)	Single	CB
Slovakia	Banking Supervision Division of the National Bank of Slovakia, Financial Market Authority (FMA)	Multiple	CB
Uruguay	Central Bank of Uruguay	Single	CB
Venezuela	Superintendent of Banks and Other Financial Institutions	Single	NCB
Summary Characteristics for Upper Middle Income Countries		*94% Single*	*65% CB*
Lower Middle Income			
Bolivia	Bank Superintendency of Bolivia	Single	NCB
Brazil	Central Bank of Brazil	Single	CB
China	China Banking Regulatory Commission	Single	NCB
Colombia	Colombia Superintendent of Banking	Single	NCB
Ecuador	Superintendency of Banks and Insurance	Single	NCB
Egypt	Central Bank of Egypt	Single	CB
El Salvador	Superintendent of the Financial System	Single	NCB
Guatemala	Guatemala Superintendent of Banks	Single	NCB
Jordan	Central Bank of Jordan	Single	CB

Morocco	Bank Al-Maghrib	Single	CB
Peru	Superintendent of Banks and Insurance	Single	NCB
Philippines	Central Bank of the Philippines	Single	CB
Romania	National Bank of Romania	Single	CB
Russia	Bank of Russia	Single	CB
South Africa	Bank Supervision Department of the South African Reserve Bank	Single	CB
Thailand	Bank of Thailand, Ministry of Finance	Multiple	CB
Turkey	Banking Regulation and Supervision Agency (BRSA)	Single	NCB
Summary Characteristics for Lower Middle Income Countries		*95% Single*	*53% CB*
Low Income			
Azerbaijan	National Bank of Azerbaijan	Single	CB
Ghana	Bank of Ghana	Single	CB
India	Board for Financial Supervision of the Reserve Bank of India	Single	CB
Kenya	Minister of Finance	Single	NCB
Kyrgyzstan	Banking Supervision Department of the National Bank of the Kyrgyz Republic	Single	CB
Moldova	National Bank of Moldova	Single	CB
Nicaragua	Superintendent of Banks and Other Financial Institutions	Single	NCB
Niger	West African Monetary Union Banking Commission	Single	CB
Nigeria[5]	Central Bank of Nigeria	Single	CB
Pakistan	State Bank of Pakistan	Single	CB
Rwanda	Central Bank of Rwanda (BNR)	Single	CB
Zimbabwe	Reserve Bank of Zimbabwe	Single	CB
Summary Characteristics for Low Income Countries		*100% Single*	*83% CB*

Source: World Bank Regulation and Supervision Survey (2003); and Neil Courtis (ed.) *How Countries Supervise their Banks, Insurers and Securities Markets 2003* (London: Central Banking Publications, 2002).

Notes:

[1] "CB" indicates that the central bank is a banking supervisory authority; "NCB" indicates that the central bank in not a banking supervisory authority.

[2] Under a "twin peaks" approach to supervision, the Australian Prudential Regulation Authority has responsibility for "prudential" (i.e., safety and soundness) supervision of banks and insurance companies; the Australian Securities and Investments Commission has responsibility for "conduct of business" (i.e., investor protection and related) supervision of banks, insurance, and securities firms."

[3] Federal level only. Each state and the District of Columbia (Washington, DC) also has a supervisory authority for banks; in some cases these state authorities are also responsible for supervising other financial services. See Courtis (2002) and Conference of State Bank Supervisors (2002) for details. Since the passage of the Gramm-Leach-Bliley Act (GLBA) in November 1999, the Federal Reserve

has served as the "umbrella regulator" of financial holding companies, which can own subsidiary commercial banks, securities firms, insurance companies, merchant banks, and other financial affiliates. See Barth, Brumbaugh, and Wilcox (2000) for a discussion of the major components of the GLBA.

[4] The Commission for Banking Supervision is governed by the General Inspectorate of Banking Supervision, whose policy-making members include regulatory authorities independent of the National Bank of Poland. These members are from the Ministry of Finance, the executive branch, the Bank Guarantee Fund, the Securities and Exchange Commission.

[5] The Financial Services Regulation Coordination Committee sets bank supervisory policy, and includes members from agencies independent of the Central Bank of Nigeria under whose auspices the Committee operates. Members come from the Securities and Exchange Commission, the Commission of Insurance, the Corporate Affairs Commission, and the Ministry of Finance.

Bank Supervisory Role of the Central Bank

Countries must also decide whether to assign responsibility for bank supervision to the central bank. As with the issue of single or multiple bank supervisors, the conceptual literature is split on the relative advantages and disadvantages of the central bank being a bank supervisor.[25] Perhaps the most strongly emphasized argument in favor of assigning supervisory responsibility to the central bank is that as a bank supervisor, the central bank will have first-hand knowledge of the condition and performance of banks. This in turn can help it identify and respond to the emergence of a systemic problem in a timely manner. Those pointing to the disadvantages of assigning bank supervision to the central bank stress the inherent conflict of interest between supervisory responsibilities and responsibility for monetary policy. The conflict could become particularly acute during an economic downturn, in that the central bank may be tempted to pursue a too-loose monetary policy to avoid adverse effects on bank earnings and credit quality, and/or encourage banks to extend credit more liberally than warranted based on credit quality conditions to complement an expansionary monetary policy.

As with the single-multiple bank supervisor debate, a useful first step in addressing the debate over the bank supervisory role of the central bank is to ascertain basic facts. Table 5 compares the bank supervisory role of the central bank in 73 countries. Almost 60 percent of those countries assign banking supervision to the central bank, including 39 countries in which the central bank is the single bank supervisory authority. The four countries that have a multiple-bank-supervisors system each assign some bank supervisory responsibility to the central bank.

[25] See Barth, Nolle, Phumiwasana, and Yago (2003, pp.73-76) for a detailed discussion of this literature.

The Scope of Supervisory Authority

Much of the discussion about consolidating financial services supervision takes as its starting point the observation that financial servicc companies are growing increasingly complex. Financial conglomerates that operate in the banking, securities, and insurance industries are among the most powerful corporations in many countries. Some have argued that a supervisor with broad scope to cover all financial services is necessary to supervise such entities effectively and, in particular, to insure that supervisory oversight of risk management by such conglomerates is not fragmented, uncoordinated, or incomplete. The most significant argument against a supervisory authority with broad scope is that it would result in an undue concentration of power that would otherwise be dispersed among several agencies. This could increase the likelihood of regulatory capture and retard financial innovation.[26]

In the face of this debate, a trend has emerged over the past two decades toward consolidating or "integrating" supervision of banking and other financial services into a single supervisory authority. Table 6, which draws on Martínez and Rose (2003), illustrates several important dimensions of this trend. First, the table shows that 26 countries have, since 1986, assigned to a single supervisory authority banking supervision and the supervision of at least one other major financial service industry (either securities or insurance); this group of "integrating" countries includes developed and developing countries. Fourteen of the countries integrating supervision have switched a single supervisory authority for all financial intermediaries, including most importantly banks, securities firms, and insurance companies. Table 6 also lists 8 other countries giving serious attention to integrating bank and other financial services supervision into a single agency. Furthermore, most of the integrating countries do not assign bank supervision to the central bank, as indicated by the asterisks in Table 6: this includes 10 of the 14 countries with a single supervisor for all financial services, and 10 of the 12 countries where bank supervision is housed with either insurance or securities industry supervision. By contrast, all of the 8 countries seriously considering integrated supervision currently assign banking supervision to the central bank.

The intense interest policy makers have shown in the issue of the appropriate structure of supervision has not been reflected in research. In particular, little systematic empirical evidence exists on how, or indeed whether, the structure and of bank supervision affects the banking industry. One recent study addressing this

[26] See Barth, Nolle, Phumiwasana, and Yago (2003) for a detailed discussion of this issue.

gap is Barth, Nolle, Phumiwasana, and Yago (2003).[27] That study summarizes the policy debates surrounding the issue, drawing on a growing conceptual literature. It also examines whether and how the structure of banking supervision affects a key dimension of bank performance – bank profitability. The results indicate, at most, a weak influence for the structure of supervision on that dimension of bank performance. The study points out, however, that the key questions of whether and how the structure of supervision affect banking system safety and soundness remain to be empirically examined.

Table 6. Countries That Have Adopted Integrated Supervision Since 1986

Single Supervisor for all Intermediaries		Single Supervisor for Banks and Insurers	Single Supervisor for Banks and Securities Firms	Considering Integrated Supervision	
Denmark*	Korea*	Australia[1]*	Finland*	Bulgaria	Slovakia
Estonia*	Latvia*	Austria*	Luxembourg*	Indonesia	Slovenia
Germany	Malta	Canada*	Mexico*	Kazakhstan	South Africa
Hungary*	Norway*	Colombia*		Poland	Ukraine
Iceland*	Singapore	El Salvador*			
Ireland	Sweden*	Malaysia			
Japan*	United Kingdom*	Paraguay			
		Peru*			
		Venezuela*			

Source: José de Luna Martínez and Thomas A. Rose, "International Survey of Integrated Supervision," in *Financial Regulation: A Guide to Structural Reform*, ed. Douglas Arner and Jan-Juy Lin (Hong Kong: Sweet & Maxwell Asia, 2003), 6; Neil Courtis, ed, *How Countries Supervise their Banks, Insurers and Securities Markets 2003* (London: Central Banking Publications, 2002); and World Bank Regulation and Supervision Survey (2003).

Note: * indicates the central bank is not assigned bank supervision responsibility.

[1] Under a "twin peaks" approach to supervision, the Australian Prudential Regulation Authority has responsibility for "prudential" (i.e., safety and soundness) supervision of banks and insurance companies; the Australian Securities and Investments

[27] Barth, Nolle, Phumiwasana, and Yago (2003) also address the issues of the scope of supervision (i.e., whether the bank supervisory authorities also have responsibility beyond the banking industry, in particular for securities and insurance firms), and supervisory independence from political influence.

Commission has responsibility for "conduct of business" (i.e., investor protection and related) supervision of banks, insurance, and securities firms."

How Do Countries Supervise Banks?

The way in which the supervisory authorities supervise banks is quite important. Indeed, unless these authorities appropriately interpret and enforce the regulations governing banks, the regulations themselves become meaningless. Perhaps more importantly, it is the supervisors who have direct contact with the banks and therefore represent the main line of defense against unsafe and unsound banking practices. Supervisory authorities therefore seek to detect and assess activities and practices that expose banks to excessive risk relative their level of capital, and to require banks to appropriately manage their risk exposures.

There are several main dimensions to bank supervision. A primary supervisory approach to assessing the riskiness of banks is through the examination process. The nature of this process is hard to quantify, and cross-country data is thin at best. However, new information on three significant aspects of supervisory practices is available that can give one an indication of the relative effectiveness of supervision. These dimensions include enforcement powers, the degree of disclosure supervisory authorities must comply with, and the independence of supervisory authorities. Information of these three dimensions is presented in Table 7.[28]

Table 7 shows that even though there is not much variation in the average level of enforcement across the different countries when grouped by income level and no variation in the average level of disclosure, there is substantial variation among the individual countries within all four income groupings. The widest range of variation in enforcement exists among the high-income countries, with the highest degree of enforcement in Australia, Japan, Luxembourg, New Zealand, Singapore, and the United Kingdom. The lowest degree of enforcement exists in Italy and the Netherlands.

As regards disclosure, the lowest degree of disclosure among all 73 countries exists in Sweden and the Czech Republic. On the other hand, the highest degree of disclosure exists in nearly one third of the countries, cutting across all four income levels in which the countries are grouped (see Table 7). Unfortunately, the World

[28] See Barth, Nolle, Phumiwasana and Yago (2003) for a measure of the degree to which supervisory authorities are subject to political influence, and Quintyn and Taylor (2002) for a discussion of the degree to which supervisors are subject to pressures from the banking industry.

Bank Regulation and Supervision Survey does not contain information on the reasons countries choose low levels of disclosure and enforcement. Clearly, however, the reasons for the differences that exist across countries merits further study, and it is important to know whether and how these aspects of supervision affect bank performance and stability.

Table 7. Supervisory Practices: International Comparisons

Country	Enforcement	Disclosure	Independence
High Income			
Australia	5	1	1
Belgium	4	1	0
Canada	2	1	1
Cyprus	1	1	1
Denmark	2	1	0
Finland	1	2	0
France	2	1	0
Germany	1	2	1
Greece	3	1	1
Hong Kong, China	4	1	1
Israel	4	1	0
Italy	0	2	0
Japan	5	1	1
Korea	4	1	0
Kuwait	4	2	1
Luxembourg	5	1	1
Netherlands	0	1	1
New Zealand	5	1	1
Norway	1	1	1
Portugal	4	1	1
Singapore	5	1	1
Slovenia	4	1	1
Spain	2	2	0
Sweden	1	0	1
Switzerland	4	1	1
United Kingdom	5	2	1
United States	4	2	1
Average	*3*	*1*	*1*
Upper Middle Income			
Argentina	3	1	0
Botswana	5	2	1
Chile	2	1	0
Czech Republic	2	0	1
Estonia	5	1	1
Hungary	5	2	1

Country	Enforcement	Disclosure	Independence
Lithuania	5	2	1
Malaysia	2	1	1
Mauritius	4	1	0
Mexico	5	2	0
Oman	5	2	0
Panama	3	1	0
Poland	3	1	0
Saudi Arabia	5	2	0
Slovakia	5	2	1
Uruguay	5	1	0
Venezuela	3	1	0
Average	*4*	*1*	*0*
Lower Middle Income			
Bolivia	3	1	0
Brazil	4	1	0
China	4	2	0
Colombia	3	2	0
Ecuador	5	2	0
Egypt	5	1	1
El Salvador	2	1	0
Guatemala	1	1	0
Jordan	4	1	1
Morocco	5	1	1
Peru	3	1	0
Philippines	5	1	0
Romania	2	1	1
Russia	3	2	0
South Africa	1	2	1
Thailand	3	2	0
Turkey	5	1	0
Average	*3*	*1*	*0*
Low Income			
Azerbaijan	3	2	0
Ghana	4	1	1
India	4	2	1
Kenya	5	2	1
Kyrgyzstan	2	2	0
Moldova	5	1	0
Nicaragua	4	1	0
Niger	1	1	1
Nigeria	5	1	1
Pakistan	5	1	1
Rwanda	5	2	1
Zimbabwe	5	1	0
Average	*4*	*1*	*1*

Source: World Bank Regulation and Supervision Survey (2003).

Notes: The Enforcement index adds one for an affirmative answer to each of the following questions: 1) Are there any mechanisms of cease and desist-type orders, whose infraction leads to the automatic imposition of civil and penal sanctions on the banks directors and managers?; 2) Can the supervisory agency order the bank's directors or management to constitute provisions to cover actual or potential losses?; 3) Can the supervisory agency suspend the directors' decision to distribute: Dividends?, Bonuses?, Management fees? The Disclosure index adds one for an affirmative answer to each of the following questions: 1) Are bank regulators/supervisors required to make public formal enforcement actions, which include cease-and desist orders and written agreements between a bank regulatory/supervisory body and a banking organization?; 2) If an infraction of any prudential regulation is found by a supervisor, must it be reported? The Independence index is one for negative response to the question: Are supervisors legally liable for their actions?

Two very important "banking environment" factors that have a bearing, ceteris paribus, on the effectiveness of supervision are the degree of government ownership in banking, and the degree of foreign ownership. Government ownership can act to undermine otherwise effective supervision of banks. Indeed, it is somewhat unclear how government bank supervisors can even be expected to properly supervise government owned banks. A fairly common practice when banks are government owned is for the government to use them as a vehicle for financing government-owned or otherwise favored enterprises and projects. Under such circumstances, it should be no surprise that the supervisory authorities are expected to play a supporting role and thus may overlook certain problems.

Foreign ownership can be a two-edged sword. A large foreign banking presence may provide host country supervisors with additional challenges in terms of developing a comprehensive understanding of foreign banks' operations, and jurisdictional tensions may arise; but foreign banks may also "import" effective supervision, in that they may be supervised by the home country supervisor, which may adhere to best practices in supervision, and in effect "compete up" the overall level of supervision in the host country. The increased globalization of banking, moreover, raises questions as to whether a transnational supervisor is more appropriate than a national supervisor.

Table 8 shows that two-thirds of the 71 countries for which data are available have some government ownership of banks (26 countries have no government owned banks). For those countries with government ownership of banks, percent of bank assets government owned range from a high of 98 percent in China to a low of 1 percent in Kenya. In only five countries with some government ownership, however, does the percentage exceed 50 percent.

Table 8. Government and Foreign Ownership of Banks: International Comparisons (Countries ranked from highest to lowest)

Country	% of Bank Assets Government-Owned
China	98
India	75
Egypt	65
Azerbaijan	58
Pakistan	54
Israel	46
Uruguay	43
Germany	42
Romania	42
Korea	40
Russia	36
Morocco	35
Argentina	32
Brazil	32
Turkey	32
Thailand	31
Poland	24
Greece	23
Portugal	23
Saudi Arabia	21
Colombia	18
Kyrgyzstan	16
Ecuador	14
Moldova	14
Switzerland	14
Chile	13
Ghana	12
Lithuania	12
Panama	12
Slovenia	12
Philippines	11
Italy	10
Hungary	9
Rwanda	7
Venezuela	7
Zimbabwe	6
Luxembourg	5
Nigeria	5
Cyprus	4
Czech Republic	4
El Salvador	4

Country	% of Bank Assets Foreign-Owned
Botswana	100
Estonia	99
New Zealand	99
Luxembourg	95
Czech Republic	90
Hungary	89
Slovakia	86
Mexico	83
Lithuania	78
Niger	73
Poland	69
Jordan	64
Panama	59
Ghana	54
Chile	47
Romania	47
United Kingdom	46
Uruguay	43
Venezuela	43
Peru	42
Kenya	39
Moldova	37
Bolivia	36
Argentina	32
Brazil	30
Korea	30
Zimbabwe	28
Kyrgyzstan	25
Mauritius	25
Colombia	22
Morocco	21
Saudi Arabia	21
Slovenia	21
Pakistan	20
Malaysia	19
Norway	19
United States	19
Portugal	18
Australia	17
Philippines	15
Cyprus	13

Country	% of Bank Assets Government-Owned
Netherlands	4
Slovakia	4
Guatemala	3
Kenya	1
Australia	0
Belgium	0
Bolivia	0
Botswana	0
Canada	0
Denmark	0
Estonia	0
Finland	0
Hong Kong, China	0
Japan	0
Jordan	0
Kuwait	0
Malaysia	0
Mauritius	0
Mexico	0
New Zealand	0
Niger	0
Norway	0
Oman	0
Peru	0
Singapore	0
South Africa	0
Spain	0
Sweden	0
United Kingdom	0
United States	0
France	n.a.
Nicaragua	n.a.

Country	% of Bank Assets Foreign-Owned
Egypt	13
El Salvador	12
Oman	12
Greece	11
Switzerland	11
Guatemala	9
Russia	9
Spain	9
South Africa	8
Ecuador	7
India	7
Japan	7
Thailand	7
Finland	6
Italy	6
Azerbaijan	5
Canada	5
Germany	4
Turkey	3
China	2
Netherlands	2
Israel	1
Denmark	0
Kuwait	0
Rwanda	0
Belgium	n.a.
France	n.a.
Hong Kong, China	n.a.
Nicaragua	n.a.
Nigeria	n.a.
Singapore	n.a.
Sweden	n.a.

Source: World Bank Regulation and Supervision Survey (2003).

In the case of foreign ownership of banks, as Table 8 shows, only three countries, Denmark, Kuwait and Rwanda, have no foreign ownership among the 67 countries for which data are available. In the remaining 64 countries, the percentages range from a high of 100 percent in Botswana to a low of 1 percent in Israel. Countries like Botswana, Estonia and New Zealand with such extremely high percentages have essentially outsourced their entire banking sectors to banks in other countries. Interestingly, the National Bank of New Zealand is owned by an Australian bank. In many cases, the foreign-ownership percentages are quite high due to the privatization and subsequent foreign purchase of previously government-owned banks.

MARKET DISCIPLINE AND CORPORATE GOVERNANCE

Although all countries regulate and supervise banks, and many countries have instituted deposit insurance systems to promote banking system safety and soundness, a fundamental conflict remains between the owners of banks and the managers and directors of banks. The "principal-agent" problem as it has come to be known starts from the premise that the goals of owners (the principals) may be significantly different from the objectives of managers and directors (the agents), who may pursue policies inconsistent with share value-maximization. To some extent such conflicts of interest can be addressed by contractual solutions, augmented by a reliance on market discipline.[29] However, high transactions costs prohibit contracts from being written to cover all possible deviations from value-maximizing behavior, and the effective application of market discipline depends on the availability of accurate, relevant, and timely information. Hence, additional rules and practices – "corporate governance" procedures – have been instituted to address gaps in contractual specifications of rights and obligations of the various claimants on firm value, and to enhance the transparency of relevant information about the firm.

The issue of corporate governance for banks is particularly important, as Caprio and Levine (2002) and Macey and O'Hara (2003) argue. Banks and other financial intermediaries themselves exert corporate governance on firms, both as creditors of firms and, in many countries, as equity holders. Indeed, as Caprio and Levine (2002) point out, in many countries, especially developing ones, where banks dominate as financial intermediaries, banks are among the most important sources of governance for firms. To the extent banks are well-managed, the allocation of capital will occur efficiently in an economy. However, if there is poor corporate governance of banks, "bank managers may actually induce firm managers to behave in ways that favor the interests of bank managers but hurt overall firm performance."[30] This in turn can hurt the performance of the economy. Indeed, Bushman and Smith (2003) make an explicit connection between corporate governance of financial intermediaries and the finance-and-economic-growth literature.

---

[29] See Bliss (2003) for a thoughtful discussion of the definition and components of market discipline.
[30] Caprio and Levine (2002, p. 18).

Despite the importance of this issue, "very little attention has been paid to the corporate governance of banks."[31] However, in the wake of recent well-publicized governance scandals at multinational firms headquartered in the U.S. and elsewhere, there has been a renewed interest in research on corporate governance, and this interest seems in part to have stimulated new interest in research on corporate governance for banking.[32] Conceptually, Macey and O'Hara (2003) argue that given the special nature of banking, it is worthwhile to consider as "stakeholders" constituents beyond shareholders. Because banks' liabilities, especially to depositors, play such a crucial role in the economy, Macey and O'Hara argue that "bank directors should owe fiduciary duties to fixed claimants as well as to equity claimants."[33] In a complementary vein, Caprio and Levine (2002) explain that there are four sources of governance for banks: "equity holders, debt holders, the competitive discipline of output markets, and governments."[34] Each of these constituents therefore has an interest in effective corporate governance for banks.

An important dimension of corporate governance is the degree of transparency that exists for the operations of a firm. One key to the provision of accurate information is the use of accurate accounting standards. Currently, a major obstacle to the application of a single, well-recognized set of accounting practices is that there are several major alternatives employed across the globe (as well as a number of local, country-specific accounting standards that are difficult or impossible for stakeholders and potential investors to "translate" into terms similar to one of the major global standards). Table 9, using new data from the World Bank Regulation and Supervision Survey 2003, illustrates the diversity in the application of accounting standards across countries.

---

[31] Macey and O'Hara (2003, p. 91). See also Caprio and Levine (2002, p. 18) , and Adams and Mehran (2003, p. 123). Note also that in some countries the issue of corporate governance of banks and other financial institutions has recently captured renewed attention from policy makers and regulatory authorities. For example, in the United States, the Sarbanes-Oxley Act of 2002 deals extensively with legal requirements aimed at enhancing the quality of corporate governance in nonfinancial and financial firms. See also Office of the Comptroller of the Currency (2003) for a federal regulatory perspective on corporate governance practices for banks.

[32] See Shleifer and Vishny (1997) for a comprehensive and thoughtful survey of research on corporate governance. Macey and O'Hara (2003) discuss the emerging literature on corporate governance for banks.

[33] Macey and O'Hara (2003, p. 102). Adams and Mehran (2003, p. 124) add at least one more constituent. They argue that "the number of parties with a stake in [a financial] institution's activity complicates the governance of financial institutions. In addition to investors, depositors and regulators have a direct interest in bank performance."

[34] Caprio and Levine (2002, p. 19).

The more comprehensive and accurate is information about how managers conduct the firm's business, the greater the chances that stakeholders will be effective in monitoring managers' performance. Extending recent work by Caprio and Levine (2002), Table 10 presents cross-country information on bank operations transparency: (1) the effectiveness of external audits of banks; (2) the transparency of bank financial statements practices; and (3) the evaluations by external rating agencies and incentives for creditors of the bank to monitor bank performance. An index summarizing country-specific component data on each of these three dimensions of corporate governance in banking is calculated, with higher values indicating better corporate governance measures.[35] In addition, the far right-hand column aggregates these indexes into a "Corporate Governance Index."

Table 10 shows variations in the components of corporate governance across countries. Looking at averages for the four country income groups, in general one can discern a positive relationship between the application of corporate governance measures and country income level. For example, the Financial Statement Transparency index is highest for the High Income countries, lowest for the Low Income countries, and in between for the two middle income sets. In this same vein, for the overall Corporate Governance Index, the High Income countries rank highest, and the Low Income countries rank lowest. However, the Lower Middle Income countries show on average a higher Corporate Governance

---

[35] The Corporate Governance Index is the sum of the component indexes, Strength of External Audit, Financial Statement Transparency and External Ratings and Creditor Monitoring. The Strength of External Audit index adds one for an affirmative answer to each of the following questions: 1) Is an external audit required?; 2) Are specific requirements for the extent or nature of the audit spelled out?; 3) Are auditors licensed or certified?; 4) Do supervisors receive a copy of the auditor's report?; 5) Can supervisors meet with auditors without prior approval by the bank?; 6) Are auditors required by law to communicate directly to the supervisory agency any presumed involvement of bank directors or senior managers in illicit activities, fraud, or insider abuse?; 7) Can supervisors take legal action against external auditors? The Financial Statement Transparency index adds one for an affirmative answer to each of the following questions: 1) Does accrued, though unpaid, interest/principal enter the income statement while the loan is still performing?; 2) Are financial institutions required to produce consolidated accounts covering all bank and any nonbank financial subsidiaries?; 3) Are off-balance sheet items disclosed to supervisors?; 4) Are off-balance sheet items disclosed to the public?; 5) Must banks disclose their risk management procedures to the public?; 6) Are bank directors legally liable if information disclosed is erroneous or misleading? In addition, this index adds one for a negative response to the following question: 7) Does accrued, though unpaid interest or principal enter the income statement while a loan is still nonperforming? The External Ratings and Creditor Monitoring index adds one for an affirmative answer to the following question: 1) Is subordinated debt allowable as a part of capital?; 2) Is subordinated debt required as a part of capital?; 3) Do regulations require credit ratings for commercial banks? The index also adds one if the top 10 banks in the country are rated by an international credit rating agency and domestic credit rating agency.

Index value than the Upper Middle Income group of countries, a pattern that holds for the External Ratings and Credit Monitoring index as well. Furthermore, although there is not much difference in the average value of the Strength of External Audit index across income groups, the Low Income group actually has a slightly higher average than the High Income group. Hence one cannot say that lower income countries uniformly employ less stringent corporate governance measures than higher income countries. Consistent with this observation, recent research by Caprio and Honohan (2003) examines the widely held notion that low income countries do not in general have the prerequisite conditions for effective market discipline, and find that there is little evidence to support that preconception.

Table 9. Bank Accounting Practices: An International Comparison

Countries Applying International Accounting Standards (IAS)	Countries Applying U.S. Generally Accepted Accounting Standards (GAAS)	Countries Applying Both	Countries Applying Neither
Azerbaijan	United States	Australia	Argentina
Bolivia		Brazil	Belgium
Botswana		Ecuador	Chile
Canada		El Salvador	China
Cyprus		Japan	Colombia
Czech Republic		Kenya	Denmark
Egypt		Mexico	Finland
Estonia		Nicaragua	France
Ghana		Nigeria	Germany
Hong Kong, China		Panama	Greece
Hungary		Philippines	Guatemala
Jordan		South Korea	India
Kuwait		Sweden	Israel
Kyrgyzstan		Switzerland	Italy
Lithuania		Thailand	Luxembourg
Malaysia			Morocco
Mauritius			Netherlands
Moldova, Republic of			Norway
New Zealand			Poland
Niger			Portugal
Oman			Russia
Pakistan			Slovenia
Peru			Spain

Countries Applying International Accounting Standards (IAS)	Countries Applying U.S. Generally Accepted Accounting Standards (GAAS)	Countries Applying Both	Countries Applying Neither
Romania			United Kingdom
Rwanda			Venezuela
Saudi Arabia			
Singapore			
Slovakia			
South Africa			
Turkey			
Uruguay			
Zimbabwe			

Source: World Bank Regulation and Supervision Survey (2003).

Table 10. Market Discipline and Corporate Governance: International Comparisons

Country	Strength of External Audit	Financial Statement Transparency	External Ratings and Creditor Monitoring	Corporate Governance Index
High Income				
Australia	5	7	2	14
Belgium	7	6	1	14
Canada	7	7	3	17
Cyprus	5	7	1	13
Denmark	7	6	3	16
Finland	6	7	2	15
France	7	5	1	13
Germany	6	5	2	13
Greece	7	6	1	14
Hong Kong, China	6	7	2	15
Israel	5	7	2	14
Italy	5	6	2	13
Japan	5	6	3	14
Korea	6	7	4	17
Kuwait	6	7	3	16
Luxembourg	7	7	1	15
Netherlands	7	6	3	16
New Zealand	5	7	3	15

Country	Strength of External Audit	Financial Statement Transparency	External Ratings and Creditor Monitoring	Corporate Governance Index
Norway	7	5	2	14
Portugal	7	5	1	13
Singapore	7	7	2	16
Slovenia	7	7	1	15
Spain	5	6	2	13
Sweden	6	6	1	13
Switzerland	7	7	1	15
United Kingdom	5	7	2	14
United States	6	6	3	15
Average	*6.15*	*6.37*	*2.00*	*14.52*
Upper Middle Income				
Argentina	6	6	4	16
Botswana	7	3	1	11
Chile	6	6	3	15
Czech Republic	5	7	1	13
Estonia	7	7	1	15
Hungary	7	6	2	15
Lithuania	5	5	1	11
Malaysia	6	7	2	15
Mauritius	6	6	2	14
Mexico	6	6	3	15
Oman	7	7	2	16
Panama	5	6	1	12
Poland	6	6	2	14
Saudi Arabia	7	7	1	15
Slovakia	7	5	1	13
Uruguay	5	6	3	14
Venezuela	7	5	2	14
Average	*6.18*	*5.94*	*1.88*	*14.00*
Lower Middle Income				
Bolivia	5	5	4	14
Brazil	6	6	3	15
China	3	5	1	9
Colombia	7	6	3	16
Ecuador	7	6	3	16
Egypt	7	7	2	16
El Salvador	7	5	3	15
Guatemala	4	5	1	10

Country	Strength of External Audit	Financial Statement Transparency	External Ratings and Creditor Monitoring	Corporate Governance Index
Jordan	7	6	1	14
Morocco	6	7	1	14
Peru	7	6	3	16
Philippines	3	7	1	11
Romania	5	5	2	12
Russia	5	6	2	13
Thailand	6	5	2	13
South Africa	7	7	1	15
Turkey	7	7	1	15
Average	*5.82*	*5.94*	*2.00*	*13.76*
Low Income				
Azerbaijan	6	5	2	13
Ghana	5	5	1	11
India	6	5	1	12
Kenya	7	7	1	15
Kyrgyzstan	4	6	1	11
Moldova	7	5	2	14
Nicaragua	6	5	2	13
Niger	7	6	1	14
Nigeria	6	6	2	14
Pakistan	7	6	2	15
Rwanda	7	5	0	12
Zimbabwe	6	6	2	14
Average	*6.17*	*5.58*	*1.42*	*13.17*

Source: World Bank Regulation and Supervision Survey (2003); and Caprio and Levine (2002).

Notes: The Corporate Governance Index is the sum of the component indexes, Strength of External Audit, Financial Statement Transparency and External Ratings and Creditor Monitoring. The Strength of External Audit index adds one for an affirmative answer to each of the following questions: 1) Is an external audit required?; 2) Are specific requirements for the extent or nature of the audit spelled out?; 3) Are auditors licensed or certified?; 4) Do supervisors receive a copy of the auditor's report?; 5) Can supervisors meet with auditors without prior approval by the bank?; 6) Are auditors required by law to communicate directly to the supervisory agency any presumed involvement of bank directors or senior managers in illicit activities, fraud, or insider abuse?; 7) Can supervisors take legal action against external auditors? The Financial Statement Transparency index adds one for an affirmative answer to each of the following questions: 1) Does accrued, though unpaid, interest/principal enter the income statement while the loan is still performing?; 2) Are financial institutions required to produce consolidated accounts covering all bank and any nonbank financial subsidiaries?; 3) Are off-balance sheet items disclosed to supervisors?; 4) Are off-balance sheet items disclosed to the public?; 5) Must banks disclose their risk management procedures to the public?; 6) Are bank directors legally liable if information disclosed is erroneous or misleading? In addition, this index adds one for a negative response to the following question: 7) Does accrued, though unpaid interest or principal enter the income statement while a loan is still nonperforming? The External Ratings and Creditor Monitoring index adds one for an affirmative answer to the following question: 1) Is subordinated debt allowable as a part of capital?; 2) Is subordinated debt required as a part of capital?; 3) Do regulations require credit ratings for commercial banks? The index also adds one if the top 10 banks in the country are rated by an international credit rating agency and domestic credit rating agency.

RISK MANAGEMENT AND BANK REGULATION AND SUPERVISION

In recent years, dramatic changes have occurred in how bank risk is measured and managed. Advances in telecommunications and information processing, as well as the emergence of sophisticated "financial engineering" have allowed banks and other financial institutions to enhance their ability to assess and price risk. In addition, perceived deficiencies with international capital requirements, as embodied in the Basel Capital Accord of 1988 ("Basel I"), have provided great incentives for banks to develop ever-sophisticated risk management models.[36] In particular, much of the current interest in fine tuning credit risk measurement models has been fueled by objections to Basel I capital rules and the development of the New Basel Capital Accord ("Basel II"), which more closely links capital charges to the credit risk exposure for individual retail, commercial, sovereign, and inter-bank credits. This section will briefly describe bank internal risk assessment models, including the traditional credit scoring system and the recent Value at Risk (VAR) models, and then describe how new financial products, such as derivatives and credit derivatives, have been used to by banks to manage risk.

Credit Scoring System –The Traditional Approach

A credit scoring system can be found in virtually all types of credit analysis, from consumer credit to commercial loans. The idea is essentially to pre-identify certain key factors that determine and probability of default and combine or weigh them into a quantitative score. In some cases, the score can be literally interpreted as a probability of default; in others, the score can be used as a classification system: it places a potential borrower into either a good or a bad group, based on a core and a cut-off point. Four econometric models has been used in credit scoring systems. They are (1) the linear probability model, (2) the logit model, (3) the probit model, and (4) the discriminant analysis model. Mester (1997) documents

[36] See section III.E.1. below for an explanation of Basel I, observations about its deficiencies, and a summary of Basel II.

the widespread use of credit-scoring models: 97 percent of banks use credit scoring to approve credit card applications, whereas 70 percent of the banks use credit scoring in their small business lending.

Value At Risk (VAR) – Modern Approach

Essentially VAR models seek to measure the minimum loss (of value) on a given asset or portfolio over a given time period at a given confidence level (e.g., 95 percent, 97.5 percent, and 99 percent). While the traditional credit scoring approach focuses on measuring credit risk for individual assets, VAR is particularly powerful in assessing the risk exposure for a portfolio of assets because it takes into account the correlation among different assets.

Credit Derivatives

Credit derivatives are designed to transfer the credit risk on portfolios of bank loans or debt securities from banks to non-banks, particularly insurance companies. There are four individual instruments. They are (1) credit options, (2) credit swaps, (3) credit forwards, and (4) credit securitizations. There has been an explosive growth in the use of credit derivatives in recent years. Market participants estimate that the world market in credit derivatives is doubling in size each year (Saunders, 2002).

The revolution in finance and risk management has imposed new challenges on regulatory and supervisory authorities. Given the increased sophistication and complexity of bank assets and risk management techniques, supervisory authorities need to develop and maintain expertise sufficient to evaluate banks' practices. More importantly, the wide-spread use of derivatives may have both positive and negative consequences for global financial market stability. By allowing banks to hold more diversified credit portfolios, the use of credit derivatives reduces bank vulnerability to systemic shocks. Moreover, credit is more available and the likelihood of credit crunches is reduced when lenders can use credit derivatives to transfer the credit risk of loans that they originate. However, this may create a wedge between borrower and lender, thereby hampering monitoring and restructuring activities. Additionally, by dispersing credit risk throughout the financial system, the impact of those shocks is more broadly felt, thereby increasing systemic risk exposure (Rule, 2001).

CROSS-BORDER ISSUES

International Cooperation in Banking Regulation and Supervision: The Basel Committee on Banking Supervision

Increasing globalization of financial services industries has caused national supervisory authorities to recognize the need for, and desirability of, international cooperation in regulation and supervision. The most significant step in this direction for the banking industry was the establishment in 1974 of the Basel Committee on Banking Supervision ("Basel Committee") by the Group of Ten countries.[37] The Basel Committee is composed of representatives from member countries' bank supervisory agencies, and focuses on formulating broad supervisory standards, guidelines, and statements of best practices. It does not have any formal supranational authority, nor do its policies have any legal force. Nevertheless, its recommendations have, from its inception, had a significant impact on bank regulation and supervision not only in the member countries, but throughout the rest of the world. Two of its initiatives in particular have had a far-reaching impact on banking systems across the globe: the Basel Capital Accord, and the Core Principles for Effective Banking Supervision.

Basel Capital Accord

"The" Basel Capital Accord has two incarnations: the original Basel Capital Accord ("Basel I"), and the proposed New Basel Capital Accord ("Basel II").[38] Basel I was adopted by the Basel Committee in 1988 with two primary objectives in mind. First, Basel Committee members were concerned about the long-term decline in bank capital, and hence Basel I was designed to increase bank capital and reduce credit risk. Secondly, required capital levels in member countries (and elsewhere around the world) varied widely, giving rise to charges of unfair competitive advantage accruing to banks in countries with lower capital requirements. Basel I sought to "level the playing field" in this respect.

There are three main elements to Basel I. The first is a system of assigning risk weights to banks' assets. For example, commercial loans are weighted at 100 percent, whereas OECD inter-bank deposits, which are considered less risky, are

[37] The Group of Ten (G-10) countries include Belgium, Canada, France, Germany, Italy, Japan, the Netherlands, Sweden, the United Kingdom, the United States and, since 1984, Switzerland. In addition to the G-10 countries, Basel Committee member countries include Luxembourg and Spain.

[38] The descriptions of Basel I and the new Basel Capital Accord ("Basel II") draw heavily on Palia and Porter (2003), and Board of Governors of the Federal Reserve System (2003).

weighted at 20 percent. The second element is a system for converting off-balance sheet items to equivalent balance sheet items for the purpose of assigning risk weights. Third, the Accord specifies acceptable components of "regulatory capital," in response to the situation where differing definitions for regulatory capital had been used by different countries. Components include equity, loan-loss reserves, subordinated debt, and several other items.[39] Basel I specifies that a bank maintain regulatory capital equal to at least 8 percent of the value of risk-weighted assets. Originally, Basel I assessed capital mainly in relation to credit risk (the risk of loss due to the failure of a counterparty to meet its obligations), but in 1996 the Accord was amended to take account of market risk as well (i.e., the risk of loss due to a change in market prices, such as equity prices or interest rates or exchange rates).

Most observers agree that Basel I represented an improvement over the widely differing capital standards that existed across the world prior to its adoption. Nevertheless, since its adoption by Basel Committee countries in 1988 (and most other countries in subsequent years), many bankers, analysts, and even supervisory authorities have pointed out significant shortcomings. Two deficiencies in particular have been widely decried.[40] First, the risk-weighting scheme has been judged to be too simplistic. As a consequence, loans assigned the same risk weights (e.g., two different commercial loans) can vary significantly in credit quality, and therefore calculated capital ratios can give a misleading picture of a bank's capital adequacy relative to risks. Second, the limited differentiation among degrees of risk creates incentives for "capital arbitrage" by banks. Banks sell, securitize, or otherwise avoid holding assets for which the regulatory capital requirement is higher than what the market requires, while at the same time retaining and seeking to acquire assets for which the regulatory capital requirement is lower than what the market would require. Hence, even though banks technically comply with Basel I rules, they end up holding too little capital.

As a result of such criticisms, the Basel Committee in 1999 began the process of fashioning and adopting the New Basel Capital Accord ("Basel II"). After extensive Committee work and banking industry comment, the final accord is to be released by midyear 2004, and it is proposed that member countries fully implement it by year-end 2006.[41] Basel II is composed of three complementary

[39] See Palia and Porter (2003, p. 226) for a detailed explanation of the components of regulatory capital.

[40] See Palia and Porter (2003, p. 228) for a more comprehensive critique of Basel I.

[41] The development of Basel II has gone through several phases, including issuance of several Consultative Papers and Quantitative Impact Studies. As recently as September 2003, the date for the issuance of the final version of the accord was set for year-end 2003, but intense debate among Basel Committee members resulted in an extension of this date to no later than midyear

"pillars." Pillar 1 deals with minimum capital requirements, but seeks to address deficiencies in Basel I; a summary of key elements of pillar 1 is given below. Pillar 2 addresses enhanced supervisory oversight, emphasizing that supervisory reviews should by guided by the following principles: 1) banks must be able to assess their capital in relation to their risk profile; 2) supervisors should evaluate banks' internal capital adequacy assessments and strategies; 3) supervisors should have the ability to require banks to hold capital in excess of the minimum; and 4) supervisors should intervene at an early stage to prevent capital from falling below the minimum levels. Pillar 3 aims to complement these activities by encouraging better market discipline through more disclosure.

Pillar 1 encompasses several significant differences from Basel I, and includes a number of different application options. Figure 4 summarizes the similarities and differences between pillar 1and capital requirements under Basel I. The 8 percent minimum capital requirement, and the definition of regulatory capital remain unchanged, but the measurement of risk exposure (the denominator in the calculation of the minimum capital requirement) changes in significant ways (although the measurement of market risk remains unchanged). Two key changes in the measurement of risk exposure include substantive changes in the treatment of securitization, and taking explicit account of operational risk.[42]

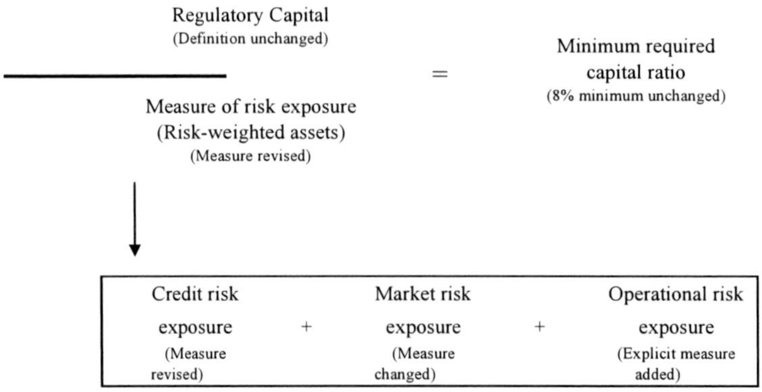

Source: Federal Reserve Bulletin, September 2003.

Figure 4. Proposed Changes to Elements of the Capital Ratio under Basel II

2004. See www.bis.org for detailed information on Basel II, including the proposed implementation schedule.

42 Securitization was a relatively new technique when Basel I was conceived, and as a consequence it "was not fully contemplated by Basel I" (Board of Governors of the Federal Reserve System [2003, p.398]). Operational risk is the risk of loss resulting from inadequate or failed internal processes, people, or systems, or from external events

In the application of pillar 1 capital ratio calculations, Basel II outlines several options for measuring credit risk and operational risk. There is a standardized approach for calculating credit risk, similar to the Basel I process where bank assets are categorized and then assigned fixed risk weights, although under Basel II there are more risk categories. Alternatively, credit risk can be calculated by either of two internal-ratings-based (IRB) approaches. Under the IRB approaches, banks evaluate the elements of credit risk for their assets. Subsequently, risk weights, and hence capital requirements, would be determined by a combination of bank-provided quantitative inputs and supervisor-provided formulas. Under the somewhat simpler "foundation" IRB approach, a bank determines each loan's probability of default, and the supervisor provides the other risk calculation inputs. Under the "advanced" IRB approach, the bank determines all the risk calculation inputs, though the supervisor validates the bank's procedure. Basel II also outlines a menu of simpler-to-more-complex processes for calculating operational risk. At the most complex end of the spectrum is the "advanced measurement approach" (AMA), designed specifically for internationally active banks, which are likely to have significant operational risk exposure. The AMA approach builds on banks' own increasingly sophisticated internal assessment techniques.[43]

Despite general agreement that Basel II represents progress in addressing shortcomings in Basel I, there is substantial debate about possible shortcomings.[44] Significantly, one aspect of Basel II has to some extent pitted banks in developed and developing countries against each other. Some observers argue in particular that it is possible that, rather than making the international playing field more level, Basel II actually further "tilts" the banking playing field against less sophisticated banks unable to take advantage of opportunities that may accrue to more sophisticated banks able to use complex internal ratings methodologies allowed under the advanced IRB approach for calculating credit risk, and the AMA approach for calculating operational risk. Developing countries are more likely to have less sophisticated banks, and hence policy makers and bankers in some developing countries argue that their banking industries will be at a competitive disadvantage under Basel II.[45] For this reason and others, supervisory

---

[43] See http://www.bis.org/publ/bcbsca.htm for Basel II documents detailing the processes for calculating credit risk and operational risk.

[44] Palia and Porter (2003, pp. 229-30), for example, compare criticisms of the "seven sins" of Basel II to those frequently cited for Basel I.

[45] See, e.g., Palia and Porter (2003, pp. 229-30).

authorities in some developing countries, including India and China, have announced that their banks will not be required to comply with Basel II.[46]

Core Principles for Effective Banking Supervision

In addition to its specific focus on bank capital adequacy, the Basel Committee has committed itself to identifying and publicizing fundamental principles and best practices in banking supervision. Since its inception, it has issued guidance in this respect for the consideration of supervisory authorities around the world. Among the most notable of these documents are the 1975 "Concordat" and its 1983 revision dealing with the supervision of internationally active banks, the 1992 "Minimum Standards", and the 1996 *Supervision of Cross-Border Banking.*[47]

Table 11. Key International Standards for Sound Financial Systems

Area	Key Standard	International Issuing Body
Financial Regulation and Supervision		
Banking Supervision	Core Principles for Effective Banking Supervision	Basel Committee on Banking Supervision
Securities Regulation	Objectives and Principles of Securities Regulation	International Organization of Securities Commissions
Insurance Supervision	Insurance Core Principles	International Association of Insurance Supervisors
Institutional and Market Infrastructure		
Insolvency	Principles and Guidelines on Effective Insolvency and Creditor Rights Systems	World Bank
Corporate Governance	Principles of Corporate Governance	Organization for Economic Cooperation and Development
Accounting	International Accounting Standards (IAS)	International Accounting Standards Board
Auditing	International Standards on Auditing (ISA)	International Federation of Accountants
Payment and Settlement	Core Principles for Systemically Important Payment Systems	Committee on Payment and Settlement Systems

46 Holland and Baglole (September 25, 2003, pp. 50-51).

47 Complete titles for the 1975 Concordat, the 1983 Revised Concordat, and the Minimum Standards are, respectively, the *Report on the Supervision of Banks' Foreign Establishments*, *Principles for the Supervision of Banks' Foreign Establishments*, and *Minimum Standards for the Supervision of International Banking Groups and Their Cross-Border Establishments*.

Market Integrity	The Forty Recommendations of the Financial Action Task Force on Money Laundering	Financial Action Task Force
Macroeconomic Policy and Data Transparency		
Monetary and Financial Policy Transparency	Code of Good Practices on Transparency in Monetary and Financial Policies	International Monetary Fund
Fiscal Policy Transparency	Code of Good Practices on Fiscal Transparency	International Monetary Fund
Data Dissemination	Special Data Dissemination Standard, General Data Dissemination System	International Monetary Fund

Source: Financial Stability Forum (2001).

Perhaps the single most influential guidance the Basel Committee has composed is the 1997 *Core Principles for Effective Banking Supervision* (the "Core Principles"). Written in the wake of the BCCI scandal, and amid emerging banking crises of the mid-to-late 1990s, the primary motivation for the codification of the Core Principles was to provide supervisory authorities and bankers and their investors with broad-based yet comprehensive thinking about the basic elements necessary for ensuring banking system safety and soundness. The 1997 Core Principles document has helped shape subsequent guidance issued under the auspices of the Bank for International Settlement, including guidance in such areas as payment system stability and electronic banking risk management.[48] Additionally, the Basel Committee's Core Principles has taken its place alongside, and in a number of cases has influenced the development of, other international standards for financial systems (listed in Table 11).

The Core Principles comprise 25 basic principles that need to be in place for a supervisory system to be effective. These principles cover the fundamental authority bank supervisors need to effectively do their job, and emphasize the importance of supervisory independence from political influence; licensing issues and powers for supervisors; appropriate and effective methods of supervision, including information needs of supervisors; and basic elements of prudential regulations and rules for banks. Box 1 provides a synopsis of the Core Principles.

In addition to helping policy makers design and improve their bank supervisory systems, an important role for the Core Principles has been in their use in the joint International Monetary Fund – World Bank Financial Sector

[48] See, for example, *Core Principles for Systemically Important Payment Systems* (Committee on Payment and Settlement Systems, January 2001), and *Risk Management Principles for Electronic Banking* (Basel Committee, July 2003).

Assessment Program (FSAP). Under this program, begun in 1999, the financial soundness of countries is assessed relative to a broad set of prudential and macroeconomic variables. A key aspect of any assessment is an evaluation of the degree to which a country's bank supervisory system complies with the Core Principles.[49] Importantly, complete compliance with the Core Principles is relatively rare, even among developed economies, as a recent report by the IMF indicates.[50] Specifically, Table 12 shows that, while 32 of 36 developing countries for which an FSAP has been completed complied with 15 or fewer of the Core Principles, less than half (4 of 9) of the advanced economies complied with all or most of the Core Principles. Hence, although there is widespread agreement that the design of the Basel Core Principles is a beneficial outcome of international cooperation by bank supervisory authorities, countries across all income classes need to strive for better implementation of best practices for bank supervision.

Box 1. Core Principles for Effective Banking Supervision

The Basel Core Principles comprise 25 basic principles that need to be in place for a supervisory system to be effective. The Principles relate to:

Objectives, autonomy, powers and resources
CP 1 is divided into six parts:
CP 1.1 deals with the definition of responsibilities and objectives for the supervisory agency.
CP 1.2 deals with, skills, resources and independence of the supervisory agency.
CP 1.3 deals with the legal framework.
CP 1.4 deals with enforcement powers
CP 1.5 requires adequate legal protection for supervisors.
CP 1.6 deals with information sharing.

Licensing and structure
CP 2 deals with permissible activities of banks.
CP 3 deals with licensing criteria and the licensing process.
CP 4 requires supervisors to review, and have the power to reject, all significant transfers of ownership in banks.
CP 5 requires supervisors to review major acquisitions and investments by banks.

Prudential regulations and requirements
CP 6 deals with minimum capital adequacy requirements. For internationally active banks, these must not be less stringent than those in the Basel Capital Accord.

[49] For explanations and assessments of the FSAP see Sundararajan et al. (2001) and Ingves and Carson (2003).
[50] Calari and Ingves (2002).

CP 7 deals with the granting and managing of loans and the making of investments.
CP 8 sets out requirements for evaluating asset quality, and the adequacy of loan loss provisions and reserves.
CP 9 sets forth rules for identifying and limiting concentrations of exposures to single borrowers, or to groups of related borrowers.
CP 10 sets out rules for lending to connected or related parties.
CP 11 requires banks to have policies for identifying and managing country and transfer risks.
CP 12 requires banks to have systems to measure, monitor and control market risks.
CP 13 requires banks to have systems to measure, monitor and control all other material risks.
CP 14 calls for banks to have adequate internal control systems.
CP 15 sets out rules for the prevention of fraud and money laundering.

Methods of ongoing supervision
CP 16 defines the overall framework for on-site and off-site supervision.
CP 17 requires supervisors to have regular contacts with bank management and staff, and to fully understand banks' operations.
CP 18 sets out the requirements for off-site supervision.
CP 19 requires supervisors to conduct on-site examinations, or to use external auditors for validation of supervisory information.
CP 20 requires the conduct of consolidated supervision.

Information requirements
CP 21 requires banks to maintain adequate records reflecting the true condition of the bank, and to publish audited financial statements.

Remedial measures and exit
CP 22 requires the supervisor to have, and promptly apply, adequate remedial measures for banks when they do not meet prudential requirements, or are otherwise threatened.

Cross-border banking
CP 23 requires supervisors to apply global consolidated supervision over internationally active banks.
CP 24 requires supervisors to establish contact and information exchange with other supervisors involved in international operations, such as host country authorities.
CP 25 requires that local operations of foreign banks are conducted to standards similar to those required of local banks, and that the supervisor has the power to share information with the home country supervisory authority.

Source: Cesare Calari and Stefan Ingves, "Implementation of the Basel Core Principles for Effective Banking Supervision, Experiences, Influences, and Perspectives," International Monetary Fund and World Bank, (September 2002), 13.

Table 12. Compliance with Core Principles

Number of Core Principles Complied With	Number of Countries	Composition of Complying Countries		
		Advanced Economies	Transitional Economies	Developing Economies
26-30[1]	5	4	1	0
21-25	5	2	0	3
16-20	6	1	4	1
11-15	12	1	2	9
6-10	11	1	3	7
0-5	21	0	5	16
Total	*60*	*9*	*15*	*36*

Source: Cesare Calari and Stefan Ingves, "Implementation of the Basel Core Principles for Effective Banking Supervision, Experiences, Influences, and Perspectives," International Monetary Fund and World Bank, (September 2002), Table 3, 13.

Notes:
[1] Although there are 25 Basel Core Principles, the joint IMF and World Bank Financial Sector Assessment Program evaluates countries according to six distinct components within Principle One; hence, for purposes of this table, countries' compliance with 30 Principles are counted (24 "Core Principles" plus 6 separate components of Principle One).

Offshore Financial Centers

Offshore financial centers (OFCs) have posed special regulatory and supervisory challenges since their emergence in the 1960s and 1970s. OFCs exist in large part because they offer financial market participants tax, regulatory, and supervisory advantages not available in their home markets. Many OFCs house predominantly legitimate financial service firms, but a few have catered to more dubious market participants. The proportion of cross-border financial activity taking place in OFCs is substantial, even if somewhat difficult to measure.[51] Furthermore, the nature of financial activities in OFCs highlights many of the challenges internationally cooperative supervisory groups face in encouraging transparency and disclosure.

[51] Figure 5a shows one measure of the significance of OFC activity, showing that as recently as the late 1990s, OFCs share of all cross-border banking claims was greater than one-third. IMF (2000, p. 4), for example, notes the lack of precise data about much non-banking financial activity conducted in OFCs.

Offshore finance is the provision of financial services by banks and other entities to non-residents. The definition of what constitutes an offshore financial center is less straightforward, and indeed a number of different categorizations of OFCs are widely recognized.[52] Nevertheless, IMF (2000) suggests a "practical definition" of an OFC, with which most observers would agree:[53]

- Financial systems with external assets and liabilities out of proportion to domestic financial intermediation;
- Relatively large numbers of financial institutions engaged primarily in business with non-residents;
- Provision of some or all of the following services: low or zero taxation, moderate or light financial regulation, banking secrecy and anonymity.

Major financial activities offered in OFCs are summarized in Box 2. Note that except for money laundering – which many OFCs do not engage in – all of the activities listed are legal. Table 13 gives structural information for 24 representative OFCs. The first column shows that in each of these jurisdictions, cross-border financial assets are many times the value of GDP, including the Cayman Islands where cross-border financial assets are 56,871 times the value of GDP. Except for banking statistics, data on financial activities and entities is generally difficult to find, but Table 13 gives estimates of the number of insurance companies, mutual funds, trust companies, and International Business Corporations (IBCs) in most of the OFCs.[54] Many offshore financial centers are known for having developed expertise in the provision of one or more financial services for non-residents. For example, Table 13 shows a preponderance of offshore insurance firms in Bermuda, which also, along with the British Virgin Islands and the Cayman Islands, is well known for offshore mutual funds.

---

[52] See, for example, IMF (2000, Table 1) for a comparison of different categorizations of OFCs.

[53] IMF (2000, p. 5).

[54] As Box 2 indicates, an IBC is a limited liability vehicle that may be used to own and operate a business, issue shares, bonds, or raise capital in other ways. Typically they are used to create complex financial structures, and frequently they are structured to minimize board of director oversight. See Financial Stability Forum (2000, Box 3) for further explanation.

Box 2. Uses of Offshore Financial Centers

Predominant vehicles through which OFCs can provide services:

Offshore Banking: Corporations or banks my open offshore banks to handle foreign exchange operations or financing needs; an individual may open an account in an offshore bank. The advantages of the offshore bank include no capital, corporate, capital gains, dividend or interest taxes, no exchange controls, and higher supervision and reporting requirements.

International Business Corporations (IBCs): IBCs are limited liability companies that may be used to operate businesses, or raise capital through issuing shares, bonds, or other instruments. In many OFCs the cost of setting up an IBC is minimal and they are exempt from all taxes.

Insurance Companies: Commercial operations may establish an insurance company in an OFC to manage risk and minimize taxes, or onshore insurance companies may establish an offshore company to reinsure certain risks in order to reduce reserve and capital requirements for the onshore company. The advantages of the OFC are favorable income/withholding/capital tax regimes and low (or weakly enforced) reserve requirements and capital standards.

Asset Management and Protection: Individuals and corporations in countries with weak economies and/or fragile banking systems may want to keep assets abroad to protect them against the possible collapse of the domestic currencies and banks, and free from any exchange controls; when confidentially is desired, then an OFC is the choice for placing the assets. Individuals who face unlimited liability in the home jurisdiction may restructure the ownership of their assets through offshore trusts to protect those assets from domestic lawsuits.

Tax Planning: Multinational firms may route transactions through OFCs to minimize total taxes through transfer pricing. Individuals can make use of favorable tax regimes in, and tax treaties with, OFCs often in the form of trusts and foundations.

Money Laundering: Proceeds from illegal activities such as drug trafficking, are processed through offshore centers to conceal the true source of the funds.

Source: Esther C. Suss, Oral H. Williams, and Chandima Mendis, "Caribbean Offshore Financial Centers: Past, Present and Possibilities for the Future," IMF Working Paper (May 2002), 5.

Table 13. Financial Activities in Offshore Financial Centers

Country/ Jurisdiction	Cross-border financial assets/GDP (percent)	*Banks*	Insurance Companies	Mutual Funds	Trust Companies	International Business Corporations (IBCs)
Aruba	75	7	29	0	0	5,000
Bahamas	5,109	212	N/A	706	107	47,000
Bahrain	66	52	70	17	0	100
Barbados	344	63	199	10	8	4,000
Bermuda	5,282	4	1,650	1,590	29	12,000
British Virgin Islands[1]	4,401	11	293	2,606	188	350,000
Cayman Islands	56,871	427	542	3,648	346	45,000
Dominica	71	5	2	0	5	8,000
Gibraltar	2,143	19	18	44	47	9,000
Grenada	18	15	6	0	11	3,000
Guernsey	7,384	69	409	585	N/A	N/A
Isle of Man	4,414	59	172	128	N/A	35,500
Jersey	6,879	62	179	368	N/A	21,000
Liechtenstein	2,750	17	21	81	N/A	N/A
Macao, SAR	54	23	24	350	N/A	12
Marshall Islands	n.a.	3	5	N/A	0	5,200
Mauritius	54	11	25	220	18	15,000
Netherlands Antilles	1,470	45	48	600	N/A	20,000
Niue[1]	18	4	0	0	0	6,000
Panama	336	80	24	N/A	46	N/A
St. Kitts & Nevis[1]	11	1	0	0	N/A	23,000
St. Vincent & Grenadines	88	20	1	4	N/A	10,000
Turks & Caicos Islands	699	8	2,572	10	N/A	16,000
Vanuatu	1,255	38	45	0	10	4,500

Source: Stefan Ingves and Carol S. Carson, "Offshore Financial Center Program: A Progress Report," Prepared by the Monetary and Exchange Affairs and Statistics Departments, International Monetary Fund (Tables 11 and 12, 2003).

Notes: n.a. and N/A signify, respectively, not available and not applicable.

[1] Cross-border financial liabilities/GDP, in percent.

Offshore financial centers emerged in the 1960s and 1970s as a response to distortionary regulations in developed economies. Such measures included interest rate ceilings, restrictions of the range of products supervised financial institutions could offer, capital controls, and high effective tax rates. Systematic data, even for the banking industry, going back that far are nonexistent, but Figure 5a shows the growing importance of offshore banking in OFCs throughout the 1980s and early 1990s. Subsequently, as onshore banking industry restrictions have been eased in major developed countries, and as the principle of consolidated supervision of all affiliates, domestic and foreign, of banking organizations began to be widely observed, OFCs have lost significant ground in offshore banking, as illustrated in Figures 5a and 5b from the mid-1990s on. Note that in 1999, the Bank for International Settlements changed the way it counts cross-border banking claims, and hence there is a discontinuity in the data series illustrated in Figures 5a and 5b. Nevertheless, the overall downward trend is evident. At the same time, although systematic data do not exist across a wide range of countries, observers agree that OFCs increased their relative worldwide share in several activities, including asset management (because substantial tax advantages persist).[55]

Despite the shift in some cross-border banking activity from less regulated OFCs to onshore jurisdictions where regulation and supervision complies with internationally recognized practices, regulatory and supervisory concerns remain about some offshore jurisdictions. For example, the Financial Action Task Force (FATF), [56] an international cooperative effort to protect financial systems from money laundering, evaluated 26 OFCs against criteria defining noncooperative behavior in the area of money laundering, and found a substantial number of violations of internationally recognized standards of cooperation.[57] Table 14 summarizes results of this evaluation for the 13 least cooperative OFCs. More broadly, international cooperative supervisory groups have identified prudential and market integrity issues related to some OFCs. These include weak supervision, poor transparency, and excessive secrecy.[58]

---

[55] On this point see IMF (2000); Financial Stability Forum (2000); Suss, Williams, and Mendis (2002); and Errico and Musalem (1999).

[56] FATF members include Australia, Austria, Belgium, Canada, Denmark, Finland, France, Germany, Greece, Hong Kong SAR, China, Iceland, Ireland, Italy, Japan, Luxembourg, the Netherlands, New Zealand, Norway, Portugal, Singapore, Spain, Sweden, Switzerland, Turkey, United Kingdom, United States, the European Commission, and the Gulf Cooperation Council. The FATF Secretariat is based at the OECD.

[57] See Suss, Williams, and Mendis (2002) for a detailed description of the FATF findings.

[58] See, e.g., Financial Stability Forum (2000).

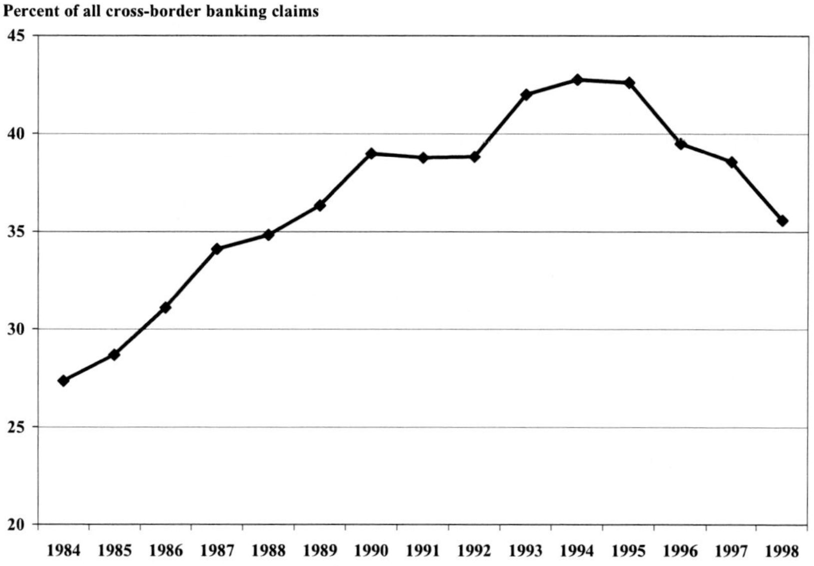

Figure 5a. Offshore Financial Centers' Share of Cross-Border Banking Claims 1984-1998

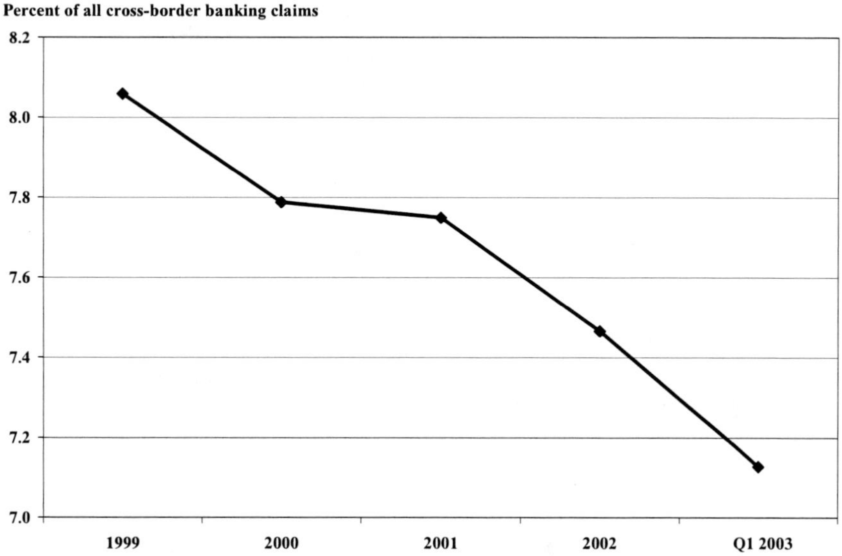

Source: Bank for International Settlements.

Figure 5b. Offshore Financial Centers' Share of Cross-Border Banking Claims 1999-2003

Table 14. Offshore Financial Centers Judged as Non-Cooperative by FATF Criteria

Country/Jurisdiction	Number of FATF Criteria Violated (Out of 25 Total)[1]
St. Kitts and Nevis	19
Marshall Islands	18
St. Vincent and the Grenadines	15.5
Cayman Islands	15
Lebanon	15
Nauru	15
Cook Islands	14
Dominica	14
Bahamas	11
Niue	11
Liechtenstein	10
Panama	8.5
Grenada	6

Source: Esther C. Suss, Oral H. Williams, and Chandima Mendis, "Caribbean Offshore Financial Centers: Past, Present and Possibilities for the Future," IMF Working Paper (May 2002), Annex II, 23.

Notes:

[1] The Financial Action Task Force (FATF) evaluates countries for the degree to which they manifest shortcomings in fighting money laundering. In particular, it has developed 25 criteria on loopholes in financial regulations, excessive secrecy provisions, and inadequate means for identifying and making available information related to financial institutions. If a country manifests a shortcoming with respect to a given criterion, FATF assigns it a value of "1" for that criterion. In some cases, FATF has determined that a country partially meets a criterion, and hence assigns a score of 0.5. Higher scores indicate weaker efforts at combating money laundering, i.e., count as being "non-cooperative."

Banking and the WTO

The World Trade Organization (WTO) General Agreement on Trade in Services (GATS) and its Annex on Financial Services (Annex), which took effect in 1999, specify the general principles that govern cross-border trade in financial services. The GATS and the Annex also specify the restrictions that may be imposed on trade in services for prudential purposes by the current 148 WTO member countries. The important point for our purposes is a country may implement regulatory measures in contravention of its GATS obligations and commitments so long as they are taken "for prudential reasons, including the protection of depositors, policy holders or persons to whom a fiduciary duty is owned by a financial service supplier, or to ensure the integrity or stability of the financial system."[59] This so-called "prudential carve-out", however, cannot be used as a means to avoid a member country's obligations and commitments. Yet, the difference between a prudential and a protective measure, both of which restrict trade in financial services, may be difficult to determine because the Annex and the GATS itself do not provide any specific guidance regarding the scope and extent of the prudential exception. Indeed, the GATS even prohibits member countries from listing prudential restrictions in their schedules of commitments. Instead, member countries retain the discretion to invoke prudential regulations to restrict cross-border trade in financial services (despite any commitments) at any time so long as the measures are taken for prudential reasons. According to Alexander (2002, p.26), "Although no formal WTO complaints have yet been brought under the Financial Services Agreement, the ambiguity which exists in the Agreement regarding the type of regulatory measures that a state may take for prudential reasons to protect its banking and financial system will likely lead to much litigation at the WTO." The reason is that "broad regulatory discretion creates an incentive for states to adopt what are ostensibly prudential measures, but is in fact non-tariff, protectionists trade measures to protect their financial services market."[60] This situation thus raises the question as to what criteria or standards can be used to determine the prudential validity of regulatory restrictions on cross-border trade in banking and other financial services.

Given the potential for disputes among countries as to what constitutes a prudential basis for restricting cross-border trade in financial services, it seems imperative that some agreement be reached regarding this issue before serious disputes actually arise. For as Alexander (2002, p.23) points out,

> "Because of the lack of guidance in defining the concept of prudential regulation or supervision, it is a strong possibility that this will be defined by panelists in WTO dispute resolution, and that panels could potentially defer to

---

[59] See Article 2(a) of the Annex on Financial Services (WTO Analytical Index) at http://www.wto.org/english/res_e/booksp_e/analytic_index_e/gats_e.htm.

[60] Alexander (2002, p. 55).

> the principles and standards adopted by international standard setting bodies, such as the Basel Committee on Banking Supervision and possibly look to the regulatory practices of major states, such as the United States and EU member states. It is questionable whether this will be a good result for the many developing countries and emerging market economies that may need differential standards of prudential regulation to address the different economic and legal structures of their financial markets."

The importance of financial markets for economic growth, development, and stability necessitates that much more effort be devoted to determining more precisely what indeed does constitute defensible and prudential restrictions on cross-border trade in financial services for the 148 WTO member countries around the world that differ in many so important respects. A one-size-fits-all approach to financial regulation and supervision certainly is not the way to resolve the prudential issue. Instead, the collection and dissemination of information on the regulation and supervision of banks in countries around the globe by the World Bank, as described in Barth, Caprio and Levine (2001b), may prove valuable in this respect. Countries that encounter disputes may defend their practices with such information by pointing to other countries acting in a similar manner. Also, the analysis of such data, as is done in Barth, Caprio and Levine (forthcoming), may result in a consensus as how best to measure the "prudential exception" to more easily help resolve any disputes that may arise among WTO member countries.

Chapter 3

DEPOSIT INSURANCE

DEPOSIT INSURANCE, SYSTEMIC STABILITY, AND MORAL HAZARD

A form of market failure that is most often discussed in the context of banks is the negative externality that exists when runs occur against solvent institutions. This problem arises when banks accept deposits that are payable on demand at par on a first-come, first-served basis, and the deposits are used to fund illiquid loans whose values are difficult for depositors to assess. Banks are subject to runs whenever depositors believe that the value of the banks' assets is insufficient to fulfill their obligations to them.

Depositors who have imperfect information or lack costly-to-obtain information may run against not only insolvent banks but also solvent banks with broadly similar portfolios, thereby creating a negative externality. Actions based upon inaccurate information could in the extreme impair the entire payments mechanism and in the process lead to asset sales at distressed prices that impair the intermediation or credit mechanism. Such situations provide a rationale for deposit insurance to prevent widespread and destructive runs on banks.

Government regulation designed to overcome one type of market failure, however, can cause problems, including other market failures. Although deposit insurance protects against widespread runs, it simultaneously eliminates the incentive of insured depositors to monitor banks. Nor does deposit insurance impose discipline on risk-taking by the owners because their losses are limited by corporate liability laws to their equity contribution. This gives rise to the moral-hazard problem that is widely associated with deposit insurance. The owners of banks have a put option on their institution's assets because of deposit insurance, and therefore have an incentive to increase the value of the option by choosing riskier portfolios and lower capital-to-asset ratios. Thus, government intervention to deal with one type of market failure can create another type of market failure.

For adequately capitalized institutions, the moral-hazard problem is virtually eliminated. As a result, minimum capital requirements have been established by law and regulation with the goal of containing the moral-hazard problem. In addition, extensive examination and supervision are designed to detect and prevent excessive risk-taking. Only through an appropriately designed deposit insurance system can its benefits exceed its costs.

INTERNATIONAL COMPARISONS OF DEPOSIT INSURANCE SYSTEMS

The inherent fragility of banks has motivated a number of nations to establish deposit insurance schemes. Such schemes are intended to assure depositors that their funds are safe by having the government guarantee that they can always be withdrawn on demand at full value. To the extent that depositors believe that the government is willing and able to keep its promise, they will have no incentive to engage in widespread runs to withdraw their funds from banks since withdrawals are honored on a first-come-first-served basis. By increasing depositor confidence, deposit insurance thus has the potential to provide for a more stable banking system.[61]

At the same time that deposit insurance increases depositor confidence, it creates a potentially serious "moral hazard" problem. When depositors believe that their funds are safe they have little, if any, incentive to monitor and police the activities of banks. When this type of depositor discipline is removed, banks are freer to engage in riskier activities. To the extent that this type of behavior is not kept in check once a country establishes a deposit insurance scheme, its banking system may still be susceptible to a crisis.

Under these circumstances, the establishment of a deposit insurance scheme is not a panacea. It provides both potential benefits and costs to a society. The

[61] See, in this regard, the seminal paper by Diamond and Dybvig (1983 and 2000). In principle, of course, a central bank by acting as a lender of last resort or by engaging in open market operations could inject liquidity into the banking system to prevent any widespread run from progressing to be point to which it disrupts economic activity.

challenge is to maximize the benefits while simultaneously minimizing the costs. For this reason, a better appreciation and understanding of deposit insurance is needed by governments and citizens in countries around the globe, particularly because ever more countries have been establishing such schemes in recent years.[62] Indeed, since the first national deposit insurance scheme was established by the United States in 1933, nearly 70 more countries have followed suit, most within the past 20 years.

There is widespread agreement that prudential regulation and supervision are particularly important for preventing banking problems once countries have established a deposit insurance scheme. Countries with such schemes must be ever more careful to contain the incentive for banks to engage in excessively risky activities funded with deposits insured by the government. For, as Hovakimian, Kane and Laeven (2002), p.23) put it: "weaknesses in risk control can generate large fiscal and social costs under an explicit insurance regime, a truth that most recent financial crises underscore." The difficult task, however, is to replace the reduced discipline of the private sector with that of the government. Nonetheless, it has done with varying degrees of success in countries around the world. The proper way to do so involves both prudential regulations and effective supervisory practices.

Skilled supervisors and appropriate regulations can help prevent banks from taking on undue risk, and thereby exposing the insurance fund to excessive loses. At the same time, however, banks must not be so tightly regulated and supervised that they are prevented from adapting to a changing financial marketplace. If this happens, banks will be less able to compete, both domestically and globally, and thus more likely to fail. The regulatory and supervisory authorities must therefore strike an appropriate balance between being too lenient and too restrictive in order to promote a safe and sound banking industry.

The appropriateness of specific regulations and supervisory practices depends upon the specific design features of a deposit insurance scheme. Some features may exacerbate moral hazard, whereas others may diminish it. A government must therefore realize that when designing a scheme it must consider the effects of various features on both depositor confidence and moral hazard. In this regard, information has recently become available describing many of the important differences among deposit insurance schemes that have been established in a wide cross-section of countries. It is thus useful to examine this "menu of deposit insurance schemes." One can thereby appreciate the ways in which these schemes

[62] In this regard, see the recent and excellent studies by Kane (2000) and Demirgüç-Kunt and Kane (2002).

differ and then try to assess those combinations of features that seem to instill depositor confidence so as to eliminate bank runs and yet satisfactorily contain the resulting moral hazard that arises when depositor discipline is substantially, if not entirely, eliminated.[63]

Approximately one third of all countries have already established deposit insurance schemes. Information on selected design features for the schemes in 73 representative countries is presented in Table 15.[64] It is quite clear from this information that there are important differences in key features across all the 48 countries that have established schemes, which includes both emerging market economies and mature economies. Moreover, the vast majority of these countries have only recently established deposit insurance for banks. Indeed, 60 percent of the countries have established their schemes within the past 20 years, and half of those countries established a deposit insurance scheme within the past decade. Even more countries, moreover, are either in the process or likely in the near future to establish a deposit insurance scheme, including Hong Kong, China, South Africa and Singapore.

One key feature of any deposit insurance scheme is the coverage limit for insured depositors. The higher the limit the more protection afforded to individual depositors. But the higher the limit, the greater the moral hazard.[65] The limits vary quite widely for countries, ranging from a low of $337 in Slovakia to a high of full coverage in Japan and Thailand. For purposes of comparison, the limit is $100,000 in the U.S. One problem with these comparisons, however, is that there are wide differences in the level of per capita income among these countries. It is therefore useful to compare the coverage limits after expressing them as a ratio to GDP per capita. Doing so one finds that Nicaragua has the highest ratio at 40, while eight countries have ratios less than 1. Clearly, ratios that are high multiples of per capita GDP are more likely to reduce the degree of discipline that depositors impose on banks.

[63] In this regard, see Hovakimian, Kane and Laeven (2002), and Demirgüç-Kunt and Detragiache (2001).

[64] For recent and comprehensive information, see Demirgüç-Kunt and Sobaci (2001). Also, see Coburn and O'Keefe (2003).

[65] The highest "coverage," and therefore the highest degree of moral hazard, arises under systems without an explicit deposit insurance scheme, but where depositors and bankers believe there is "implicit" full coverage for all deposits by the government.

Table 15. Key Features of Deposit Insurance Schemes: International Comparisons

Country[1]	Date Enacted / Revised	Coverage Limits per Account (US$)	GDP per Capita (US$)	Co-Insurance	Type of Fund (Ex-ante = Funded and Ex - post = Unfunded)	Source of Funding	Risk-Adjusted Premiums	Type of Membership
High Income								
Australia	N/A	N/A	19,019	N/A	N/A	N/A	N/A	N/A
Belgium	1974/1995	17,400	22,323	Yes	Funded	The banks	Yes	Compulsory
Canada	1967	37,984	22,343	Yes	Both	The banks	Yes	Not Compulsory
Cyprus	2000	22,637*	12,004	Yes	Both	The banks	No	Compulsory
Denmark	1988/1998	5,455	30,144	No	Funded	The banks	No	Compulsory
Finland	1969/1992/1998	25,000	23,295	No	Funded	The banks	Yes	Compulsory
France	1980/1995	79,230*	22,129	Yes	Funded	The banks	Yes	Compulsory
Germany	1966/1969/1998	21,600	22,422	Yes	Funded	The banks	Yes	Compulsory
Greece	1993/1995	21,400	11,063	No	Funded	The banks	No	Compulsory
Hong Kong, China	N/A	N/A	24,074	N/A	N/A	N/A	N/A	N/A
Israel	N/A	N/A	17,024	N/A	N/A	N/A	N/A	N/A
Italy	1987/1996	116,911*	18,788	No	Unfunded	The banks	Yes	Compulsory
Japan	1971	Full	32,601	N/A[2]	Funded	The capital of Deposit Insurance Corporation comes from both, and insurance premium comes from banks	No	Compulsory
Korea	1996	42,384*	8,917	No	Funded	Both	No	Compulsory

Table 15. Continued

Kuwait	N/A	N/A	16,048	N/A	N/A	N/A	N/A	N/A
Luxembourg	1989	17,670*	42,041	No	Unfunded	The banks	No	Compulsory
Netherlands	1979/1995	22,637*	23,701	No	Banks bear the costs of a deposit insurance protection system afterwards (ex post)	Banks, but not really funded. Banks bear the costs of a deposit insurance protection system afterwards.	No	Compulsory
New Zealand	N/A	N/A	13,101	N/A	N/A	N/A	N/A	N/A
Norway	1961/1997	277,393*	36,815	No	Funded	The banks	Yes	Compulsory
Portugal	1992/1995	28,297*	10,954	Yes	Funded	The banks	Yes	Compulsory
Singapore	N/A	N/A	20,733	N/A	N/A	N/A	N/A	N/A
Slovenia	2001	20,251*	9,443	Yes	Only when there is a need ex post	The banks	No	Compulsory
Spain	1977/1996	22,637*	14,150	Yes	Funded	The banks	No	Compulsory
Sweden	1996	28,329*	23,590	No	Funded	The government	Yes	Compulsory
Switzerland	1984/1993	21,914*	34,171	No	Unfunded	The banks	No	Not Compulsory
United Kingdom	1982/1995	100% of first £2000 and 90% of next £33,000*	24,219	Yes	Both	The banks	No	Compulsory
United States	1934/1991	100,000	35,277	No	Both	The banks	Yes	Compulsory
Upper Middle Income								
Argentina	1979/1995	10,526	7,166	No	Funded	The banks	Yes	Compulsory
Botswana	N/A	N/A	3,066	N/A	N/A	N/A	N/A	N/A
Chile	1986	2,500*	4,314	Yes	No premia is collected by the Chilean deposit insurance system	The government	No	Compulsory

Czech Republic	1994	28,297*	5,554	Yes	Funded	The banks	No	Compulsory
Estonia	1998	2,223	4,051	No	Funded	The banks	No	Compulsory
Hungary	1993	12,857*	5,097	Yes	Funded	The banks	Yes	Not Compulsory
Lithuania	1996	10,000	3,444	Yes	Funded	Both	No	Compulsory
Malaysia	N/A	N/A	3,699	N/A	N/A	N/A	N/A	N/A
Mauritius	N/A	N/A	3,750	N/A	N/A	N/A	N/A	N/A
Mexico	1986/1990	N/A[3]	6,214	There is an upper limit (400,000 Udis by 2005)	Both	Both	No, but risk adjusted fees are under study	Compulsory
Oman	1995	$52,000 subject to limit of 75% of net deposit	8,050	Depositor is insured only for RO 20,000 subject to limit of 75% of net deposit	Funded	Both	No	Compulsory
Panama	N/A	N/A	3,511	N/A	N/A	N/A	N/A	N/A
Poland	1995	Covers up to 100% for persons with deposits up to 1,000 euro and from 90% for persons with deposits between 1,000 euro up to 22,500.	4,561	Yes	Both	The banks	No	Compulsory
Saudi Arabia	N/A	N/A	8,711	N/A	N/A	N/A	N/A	N/A
Slovakia	1996	337[4]	3,786	Yes	Both	The banks	No	Compulsory
Uruguay	N/A	N/A	5,554	N/A	N/A	N/A	N/A	N/A
Venezuela	1985	6,250	5,073	No	Funded	The banks	No	Compulsory
Lower Middle Income								
Bolivia	N/A	N/A	936	N/A	N/A	N/A	N/A	N/A

Table 15. Continued

Brazil	1995	5,970	2,915	No	Funded	The banks	No	Compulsory
China	N/A	N/A	911	N/A	N/A	N/A	N/A	N/A
Colombia	1985	8,670	1,915	Yes	Funded	The banks	No	Compulsory
Ecuador	1999	7,836	1,396	Yes	Funded	The banks	Yes	Compulsory
Egypt	N/A	N/A	1,511	N/A	N/A	N/A	N/A	N/A
El Salvador	1999	6,700	2,147	No	Funded	Both	Yes	Compulsory
Guatemala	N/A	2,500	1,754	No	Funded	Both	No	Compulsory
Jordan	2000	14,104*	1,755	Yes	Funded	The banks	No	Compulsory
Morocco	N/A	5,231	1,173	Yes	Funded	The banks	No	Compulsory
Peru	1992	19,485*	2,051	No	Funded	The banks	Yes	Compulsory
Philippines	1963	1,883	912	Yes	Funded	Both	No	Compulsory
Romania	1996	3,588*	1,728	No	Funded	The banks	No	Compulsory
Russia	N/A	N/A	2,141	N/A	N/A	N/A	N/A	N/A
South Africa	N/A	N/A	2,620	N/A	N/A	N/A	N/A	N/A
Thailand	N/A	Blanket Guarantee	1,874	No	Funded	Both	No	Compulsory
Turkey	1983	35,435*	2,155	No	Funded	Both	Yes	Compulsory
Low Income								
Azerbaijan	N/A	N/A	688	N/A	N/A	N/A	N/A	N/A
Ghana	N/A	N/A	269	N/A	N/A	N/A	N/A	N/A
India	1961	2,049*	462	No	Funded	The banks	No	Compulsory
Kenya	1985	1,333	371	Yes	Funded	Both	No	Compulsory
Kyrgyzstan	N/A	N/A	308	N/A	N/A	N/A	N/A	N/A
Moldova	N/A	N/A	346	N/A	N/A	N/A	N/A	N/A
Nicaragua	N/A	19,895*	489	No	Funded	The banks	Yes	Compulsory
Niger	N/A	N/A	175	N/A	N/A	N/A	N/A	N/A
Nigeria	1988/1989	396	319	No	Funded	The banks	No	Compulsory
Pakistan	N/A	N/A	415	N/A	N/A	N/A	N/A	N/A
Rwanda	N/A	N/A	215	N/A	N/A	N/A	N/A	N/A
Zimbabwe	N/A	N/A	706	N/A	N/A	N/A	N/A	N/A

Source: World Bank Regulation and Supervision Survey (2003); *World Development Indictors*, World Bank; International Association of Deposit Insurers; and Asli Demirgüç-Kunt and Tolga Sobaci , "Deposit Insurance Around the World," *The World Bank Economic Review* 15(September 2001): 481-490.

Notes: * coverage per person

[1] Countries without explicit deposit insurance scheme include: Australia, Azerbaijan, Bolivia, Botswana, China, Egypt, Ghana, Hong Kong, China, Israel, Kuwait, Kyrgyzstan, Malaysia, Mauritius, Moldova, New Zealand, Niger, Pakistan, Panama, Russia, Rwanda, Saudi Arabia, Singapore, South Africa, Uruguay, Zimbabwe.

[2] Current Deposits, Ordinary Deposits and Specified Deposits will remain protected in full until March 31, 2005. From April 2005 onwards, the deposits referred to as "the Payment and Settlement Deposits", which satisfy the following three conditions (Bearing no interest, Deposit redeemable on demand, and provides normally required payment and settlements services.) will be protected in full. Other insured deposits (e.g. time deposits) the principal in the amount of no more than 10 million yen and interest are protected per person at each financial institution.

[3] 400,000 investment units (3.25 pesos per unit approximately). [The limit per person is divided and paid on a pro-rata basis among the number of accounts].

[4] Maximum 13,500 SKK or maximum of 40 times the average monthly wage in the Slovak Republic for the past four quarters preceding the day when the deposits became inaccessible. Compensation is provided at 90 percent of the nominal value of deposits of one depositor in one bank. With the accession of the Slovak Republic to the European Union, compensation will be provided of up to EUR 20.000,- converted to Slovak crowns, whereby the system of deposit protection in the Slovak Republic would guarantee deposits in line with deposit protection rules of the European Union.

In addition to coverage limits, countries also differ in whether coinsurance is a part of the deposit insurance scheme. This particular feature, when it is present, means that depositors are responsible for a percentage of any losses should a bank fail. Nearly 40 percent of the countries have such a feature. This is important because to the extent that depositors bear a portion of any losses resulting from a bank failure, they have an incentive to monitor and police banks. Usually, even when countries adopt coinsurance, the percentage of losses borne by depositors is capped at 10 percent. Even this relatively small percentage, however, may be enough to attract the attention of depositors when compared with the return they can expect to earn on their deposits, and thereby help to curb moral hazard.

Some countries have elected to establish an ex-ante funded scheme, whereas others have chosen to provide the funds for any losses from bank failures ex-post. Of the 48 countries with deposit insurance, only three have chosen to establish an ex-post or unfunded scheme. In this case the funds necessary to resolve bank failures are obtained only after bank failures occur. This type of arrangement may provide a greater incentive for private monitoring and policing, because everyone will know that the funds necessary to resolve problems have not yet been collected. And everyone will also know that a way to keep any funds from being collected is to prevent banks from engaging in excessively risky activities. The degree of monitoring, moreover, depends on the source of funding. In this regard, there are three alternative arrangements: public funding, private funding, or joint funding. Of these sources, private funding provides the greatest incentive for private discipline, and public funding the least. In this regard, Table 15 shows that 70 percent of the countries fund their deposit insurance schemes solely on the basis of private sources. At the same time, moreover, only two countries rely solely on public funding

In addition to those design features, there are at least two other features that must be decided upon when a country establishes a deposit insurance scheme. One is whether premiums paid by banks for deposit insurance should be risk-based. The advantage of risk-based premiums is that they potentially can be used to induce banks to avoid engaging in excessively risky activities. This would give banking authorities an additional tool to contain moral hazard. Even though, in practice it is extremely difficult to set and administer such a premium structure, Table 15 shows that one third of the countries have chosen to adopt risk-based premiums. Most countries that have adopted the schemes are careful to refer to them as differential premia systems rather than risk-based, and a common critique is that the difference between the lowest premium and the highest is quite limited.[66]

The last feature to be discussed is the membership structure of a deposit insurance scheme. A country must decide whether banks may voluntarily join or will be required to join. A voluntarily scheme will certainly attract all the weak banks. The healthy banks, in contrast, are unlikely to perceive any benefits from membership. If this happens, the funding for resolving problems will be questionable for both ex-ante and ex-post schemes. Indeed, the entire scheme may merely become a government bailout for weak banks. By requiring all banks to become members, the funding base is broader and more reliable. At the same time, when the healthy banks are members, they have a greater incentive to monitor and police the weaker banks to help protect the fund. As Table 15 shows, only Canada and Switzerland do not make membership compulsory for banks.

Although many countries at all levels of income and in all parts of the world have established deposit insurance schemes, they have not chosen a uniform

[66] Moreover, in the United States, which does have a differential premium, no premium in fact has been collected for a number of years from banks. The reason is that the relevant legislation includes a feature that stops all contributions once a certain funding ratio has been reached, which has indeed been the case.

structure. The specific design features differ widely among countries as indicated in Table 15. The fact that so many countries around the globe have suffered banking crisis over the past 20 years has generated a substantial amount of research focusing on the relationship between a banking crisis and deposit insurance. Although this type of research is still ongoing, there are currently enough studies from which to draw some, albeit tentative, conclusions about deposit insurance schemes that help promote a safe and sound banking industry.[67] They are as follows:

- Even without a deposit insurance scheme, countries have responded on occasion to banking crises with unlimited guarantees to depositors. An appropriately designed scheme that includes a coverage limit many be better able to serve notice to depositors as to the extent of their protection and thereby enable governments to avoid more costly ex-post bailouts.
- The design features of a deposit insurance scheme are quite important. Indeed, recent empirical studies show that poorly designed schemes increase the likelihood that a country will experience a banking crisis.
- Properly designed deposit insurance schemes can help mobilize savings in a country and foster overall financial development. Research has documented this important linkage but emphasizes that it only holds in countries with a strong legal and regulatory environment.
- Empirical research shows that market discipline is seriously eroded in countries that have designed their deposit insurance schemes with a high coverage limit, an ex-ante fund, the government being the sole source of funds, and only public officials as the administrators of the fund.
- Empirical research shows that market discipline is enhanced significantly in countries that have designed their deposit insurance schemes with coinsurance, mandatory membership, and private or joint administration of the fund.

[67] See Hovakimian, Kane and Laeven (2002); Kane (2000); Demirgüç-Kunt and Kane (2002); Demirgüç-Kunt and Detragiache (2001, 2000, 1998b, and 1998a); Demirgüç-Kunt, Detragiache and Gupta (2000); and Barth, Caprio and Levine (forthcoming). In the case of the U.S. savings and loan crisis in the 1980s, practices that were quite common among private insurers to help control risk-taking behavior were not adopted by the federal deposit insurer, see Barth, Bartholomew and Bradley (1991).

Chapter 4

SUMMARY AND CONCLUSIONS

The importance of the financial system in an economy can hardly be overstated, and the banking industry remains at the core of the financial system, even in countries where its credit role has diminished relative to other financial sectors. Recent changes in the nature of banking, and the frequency in the past couple of decades of costly banking crises around the world, have only heightened the interest of policy makers and industry participants in the effective regulation and supervision of banks. The task of choosing an effective bank regulatory and supervisory system is aided by an understanding of different choices countries have made in this regard. This paper's aim is to provide an overview of key trends in bank regulation and supervision in countries at all levels of income and in all parts of the world.

The study draws on recent research on important aspects of regulation and supervision, and supplements its with recent detailed cross-country data on salient aspects. These include the nature and changing role of banks in promoting economic growth, development, and economic stability; the definition of what a bank is, and restrictions on the scope of banking activities and allowable ownership arrangements; the structure and scope of bank regulatory and supervisory schemes; supervisory practices to promote safe and sound banking; market discipline and corporate governance in banking; international cooperation, standards, and practices in banking supervision; offshore banking, and potential disputes in banking arising from World Trade Organization membership; and deposit insurance schemes. A review of these issues, as well as international comparative information on these important aspects of banking regulation and supervision, can give needed perspective to debates about appropriate public policies for the banking industry.

References

Adams, Renée and Hamid Mehran. "Is Corporate Governance Different for Bank Holding Companies?" *Economic Policy Review*, Federal Reserve Bank of New York 9, Special Issue (April 2003): 123-142.

Alexander, Kern. "*The World Trade Organization and Financial Stability: The Need to Resolve the Tension Between Liberalisation and Prudential Regulation.*" Working Paper No.5, ESRC Centre for Business Research, Cambridge University (2002).

Allen, Franklin and Douglas Gale. *Comparing Financial Systems*, Cambridge. MA: The MIT Press, 2000.

Arestis, Philip and Panicos O. Demetriades. "Financial Development and Economic Growth: Assessing the Evidence." *The Economic Journal* 107 (May 1997): 783-799.

Bae, Kee-Hong, Jun-Koo Kang and Chan-Woo Lim. "The Value of Durable Bank Relationships: Evidence from Korean Banking Shocks." *Journal of Financial Economics* 64 (May 2002): 181-214.

Bank for International Settlements. *Report on the Supervision Banks' Foreign Establishments*. Basel, Switzerland, Bank for International Settlements, 1975.

Bank for International Settlements. *Principles for the Supervision Banks' Foreign Establishments*. Basel, Switzerland, Bank for International Settlements, 1983.

Bank for International Settlements. *Minimum Standards for the Supervision of International Banking Groups and Their Cross-Border Establishments*. Basel, Switzerland, Bank for International Settlements, 1992.

Bank for International Settlements. *Supervision of Their Cross-Border Banking.* Basel, Switzerland, Bank for International Settlements, 1996

Bank for International Settlements. *1997 Core Principles for Effective Banking Supervision*. Basel, Switzerland, Bank for International Settlements, 1997

Bank for International Settlements, Committee on Payment and Settlement Systems (CPSS). *Core Principles for Systemically Important Payment Systems*. Basel, Switzerland, Bank for International Settlements, 2001.

Bank for International Settlements, Basel Committee. *Risk Management Principles for Electronic Banking*. Basel, Switzerland, Bank for International Settlements, 2003.

Barth, James R., Philip F. Bartholomew and Michael G. Bradley. "Reforming Federal Deposit Insurance: What Can Be Learned from Private Insurance Practices?" *Consumer Finance Law Quarterly Report* 45 (Spring 1991).

Barth, James R., R. Dan Brumbaugh, and James A. Wilcox. "The Repeal of Glass-Steagall and the Advent of Broad Banking." *Journal of Economic Perspectives* 14 (Spring 2000): 191-204.

Barth, James R., Gerard Caprio, and Ross Levine. "Banking Systems Around the Globe: Do Regulations and Ownership Affect Performance and Stability?" in *Prudential Supervision: What Works and What Doesn't*, ed. Frederic S. Mishkin, 31-96. Chicago: University of Chicago Press, 2001a.

Barth, James R., Gerard Caprio, and Ross Levine. "The Regulation and Supervision of Banks Around the World: A New Database." in *Integrating Emerging Market Countries into the Global Financial System*, ed. Robert E. Litan and Richard Herring, *Brookings-Wharton Papers on Financial Services*, 183-240. Washington, D.C.: Brookings Institution Press, 2001b.

Barth, James R., Gerard Caprio and Ross Levine. "Bank Regulation and Supervision: What Works Best?" *Journal of Financial Intermediation*, forthcoming.

Barth, James R., Gerard Caprio and Daniel E. Nolle. "Comparative International Characteristics of Banking." in *A Companion to International Business Finance*, ed. Raj Aggarwal. Malden, MA: Blackwell Publishing, Inc., forthcoming.

Barth, James R., Steven B. Caudill, Thomas Hall and Glenn Yago. "Cross-Country Evidence on Banking Crises: Do Financial Structure and Bank Regulation Matter?" in *Bank Fragility and Regulation: Evidence from Different Countries*, Research in Financial Services: Private and Public Policy, ed. George G. Kaufman, 3-23. JAI, 2000.

Barth, James R., Luis G. Dopico, Daniel E. Nolle and James A. Wilcox. "An International Comparison and Assessment of the Structure of Bank Supervision," in *Financial Regulation: A Guide to Structural Reform*, ed. Jan-Juy Lin and Douglas Arner, 57-92. Hong Kong: Sweet & Maxwell, 2002.

Barth, James R., Daniel E. Nolle, Triphon Phumiwasana, and Glenn Yago. "A Cross-Country Analysis of the Bank Supervisory Framework and Bank

Performance." *Financial Markets, Institutions & Instruments* 12 (May 2003): 67-120. Malden, MA: Blackwell Publishing Inc.

Beck, Thorsten, Ross Levine and Norman Loayza. "Finance and the Sources of Growth." *Journal of Financial Economics* 58 (October 2000): 261-300.

Bernanke, Ben S. and Alan S. Blinder. "The Federal Funds Rate and the Channels of Monetary Transmission." *American Economic Review* 82 (September 1992): 901-921.

Besanko, David and George Kanatas. "Credit Market Equilibrium with Bank Monitoring and Moral Hazard." *Review of Financial Studies* 6 (Spring 1993): 213-232.

Bester, Helmut. "Screening vs. Rationing in Credit Markets with Imperfect Information." *American Economic Review* 75 (September 1985): 850-855.

Bishop, Matthew. "The Regulator Who Isn't There." *Capitalism and Its Troubles: A Survey of International Finance. Economist*, 16 May 2002, 12-16.

Bliss, Robert R. "Market Discipline: Players, Processes, and Purposes." Paper presented at the "Market Discipline: The Evidence across Countries and Industries," Sixth Annual Global Conference, Cosponsored by the Bank for International Settlements and the Federal Reserve Bank of Chicago, Chicago, IL, 30 October – 1 November 2003.

Bonin, John and Paul Wachtel. "Financial Sector Development in Transition Economies: Lessons from the First Decade." *Financial Markets, Institutions & Instruments* 12 (February 2003).

Boyd, John H., Chun Chang and Bruce D. Smith. "Moral Hazard Under Commercial and Universal Banking." *Journal of Money, Credit, and Banking* 30 (August 1998): 426-468.

Briault, Clive. "The Rationale for a Single National Financial Services Regulator." Financial Services Authority Occasional Paper, Series 2 (1999).

Brown, Kym and Michael Skully. "International Studies in Comparative Banking: A Survey of Recent Developments." SSRN Working Paper No. 365920, (January 2003).

Bushman, Robert M. and Abbie J. Smith. "Transparency, Financial Accounting Information, and Corporate Governance." *Economic Policy Review*, Federal Reserve Bank of New York 9, Special Issue (April 2003): 65-90.

Calari, Cesare and Stefan Ingves. "*Implementation of the Basel Core Principles for Effective Banking Supervision, Experiences, Influences, and Perspectives*." International Monetary Fund and World Bank (September 2002).

Camdessus, Michael. "The Challenges of a Sound Banking System," in *Banking Soundness and Monetary Policy*, ed. Charles Enoch and John H. Green, 535-539. Washington, D.C.: International Monetary Fund, 1997.

Caprio, Gerard and Patrick Honohan. *Finance for Growth: Policy Choices in a Volatile World.* Washington, D.C.: World Bank, 2001.

Caprio, Gerard and Patrick Honohan. "*Can the Unsophisticated Market Provide Discipline?" Paper presented at the "Market Discipline: The Evidence across Countries and Industries*," Sixth Annual Global Conference, Cosponsored by the Bank for International Settlements and the Federal Reserve Bank of Chicago, Chicago, IL, 30 October – 1 November 2003.

Caprio, Gerard and Ross Levine. "Corporate Governance in Finance: Concepts and International Observations." in *Financial Sector Governance: The Roles of the Public and Private Sectors*, ed. Robert E. Litan, Michael Pomerleano, and V. Sundararajan, 17-49. Washington, DC: Brookings Institution Press, 2002.

Claessens, Stijn, Thomas Glaessner, and Daniela Klingebiel. "*E-Finance in Emerging Markets: Is Leapfrogging Possible?*" Financial Sector Discussion Paper No. 7, World Bank (June 2001).

Claessens, Stijn, Thomas Glaessner, and Daniela Klingebiel. "*Electronic Finance: A New Approach to Financial Sector Development?*" World Bank Discussion Paper No. 431, (March 2002).

Coburn, Jane F. and John P. O'Keefe. "Risk Assessment: Results of an International Survey of Deposit Insurers." *FDIC Banking Review* 15 (June 2003): 17-35.

Conference of State Bank Supervisors. *A Profile of State Chartered Banking*, Nineteenth Edition, 2002.

Courtis, Neil, ed. *How Countries Supervise their Banks, Insurers and Securities Markets 2003*. London: Central Banking Publications, 2002.

Crockett, Andrew. Banking Supervision and Regulation: International Trends. "64th Banking Convention of the Mexican Bankers' Association," Acapulco, March 30, 2001. *http://www.bis.org/speeches/sp010330.htm*

Demirgüç-Kunt, Asli and Enrica Detragiache. "*Financial Liberalization and Financial Fragility.*" IMF Working Paper, WP/98/83, (June 1998a).

Demirgüç-Kunt, Asli and Enrica Detragiache. "*The Determinants of Banking Crises: Evidence from Developing and Developed Countries*." IMF Staff Papers 45 (March 1998b): 81-109.

Demirgüç-Kunt, Asli and Enrica Detragiache. "Monitoring Banking Sector Fragility: A Multivariate Logit Approach." *The World Bank Economic Review* 14 (May 2000): 287-307.

Demirgüç-Kunt, Asli and Enrica Detragiache. "Does Deposit Insurance Increase Banking System Stability? An Empirical Investigation." *Journal of Monetary Economics* 49 (October 2001): 1373-1406.

Demirgüç-Kunt, Asli, Enrica Detragiache and Poonam Gupta. "*Inside the Crisis: An Empirical Analysis of Banking Systems in Distress.*" World Bank Policy Research Working Paper No. 2431 (August 2000).

Demirgüç-Kunt, Asli and Edward J. Kane. "Deposit Insurance Around the Globe: Where Does It Work?" *Journal of Economic Perspectives* 16 (Spring 2002): 175-196.

Demirgüç-Kunt, Asli and Ross Levine, eds. *Financial Structure and Economic Growth*. Cambridge: The MIT Press, 2001.

Demirgüç-Kunt, Asli and Tolga Sobaci. "Deposit Insurance Around the World." *The World Bank Economic Review* 15 (September 2001): 481-490.

Demirgüç-Kunt, Asli and Vojislav Maksimovic. "Funding Growth in Bank-Based and Market-Based Financial Systems: Evidence from Firm-Level Data." *Journal of Financial Economics* 65 (September 2002): 337-363.

Diamond, Douglas W. "Financial Intermediation and Delegated Monitoring." *Review of Economic Studies* 51 (July 1984): 393-414.

Diamond, Douglas W. and Philip H Dybvig. "Bank Runs, Deposit Insurance, and Liquidity." *Federal Reserve Bank of Minneapolis Quarterly Review* 24 (Winter 2000): 4-23.

Diamond, Douglas W. and Philip H Dybvig. "Bank Runs, Deposit Insurance, and Liquidity." *Journal of Political Economy* 91 (June 1983): 401-419.

Edwards, Franklin R. "Banks and Securities Activities: Legal and Economic Perspective on the Glass-Steagall Act." in *The Deregulation of Banking Securities Activities*, ed. Lawrence G. Goldberg and Lawrence J. White, 273-294. Lexington, MA: Lexington Books, 1979.

Easterbrook, Frank H. "Two-Agency Cost Explanation of Dividends." *American Economic Review* 74 (September 1984): 650-659.

Errico, Luca and Alberto Musalem. "*Offshore Banking: An Analysis of Micro- and Macro-Prudential Issues*." IMF Working Paper, International Monetary Fund (January 1999).

Fama, Eugene F. "What's Different about Banks?" *Journal of Monetary Economics* 15 (January 1985): 29-39.

Federal Reserve Board. "Capital Standards for Banks: The Evolving Basel Accord." *Federal Reserve Bulletin* (September 2003).

Financial Stability Forum. *Report of the Working Group on Offshore Centres*. Basel, Switzerland: Financial Stability Forum, 2000.

Financial Stability Forum. *International Standards and Codes to Strengthen Financial Systems*. Basel, Switzerland: Financial Stability Forum, 2001.

Freixas, Xavier and Jean-Jacquees Laffont. "Optimal Banking Contracts, in *Essays in Honor of Edmond Malinvaud: Volume 2: Macroeconomics*, ed. Paul Champsaur, et al., 33-61. Cambridge, MA: M.I.T. Press, 1990.

Gan, Jie. "*Financing Choices of Banks: the Role of Non-Binding Capital Requirements*." Hong Kong University of Science and Technology Working Paper (2003a).

Gan, Jie. "*The Value of Banking Relationship: Evidence an Exogenous Shock to Bank Health.*" Hong Kong University of Science and Technology Working Paper (2003b).

Gibson, Michael S. "Can Bank Health Affect Investment? Evidence from Japan." *Journal of Business* 68 (July 1995): 281-308.

Goldsmith, Raymond W. *Financial Structure and Development*. New Haven, CT: Yale University Press, 1969.

Goodhart, Charles. "*Financial Integration and Prudential Control Segmentation: What Kind of Coordination Does Prudential Policy Need in the Integrated European Financial Market?*" Unpublished paper, Financial Markets Group, London School of Economics (2002).

Haubrich, Joseph G. and João A. Santos. "Alternative Forms of Mixing Banking with Commerce: Evidence from American History." *Financial Markets, Institutions & Instruments* 12 (May 2003): 121-164. Malden, MA: Blackwell Publishing Inc.

Holland, Tom and Joel Baglole. "Asia Faces a Stark Choice." *Far Eastern Economic Review* (September 25, 2003):50-51.

Holmstrom, Bengt and Jean Tirole. "Financial Intermediation, Loanable Funds, and the Real Sector." *Quarterly Journal of Economics* 112 (August 1997): 663-691.

Hoshi, Takeo, David Scharfstein and Kenneth Singleton. "Japanese Corporate Investment and Bank of Japanese Guidance of Commercial Bank Lending." in *Japanese Monetary Policy*, ed. Kenneth Singleton, 63-94. Chicago: University of Chicago and NBER,1992.

Hovakimian, Armen, Edward J. Kane and Luc Laeven. "*How Country and Safety-Net Characteristics Affect Bank Risk-Shifting.*" NBER Working Paper No. w9322 (November 2002).

Ingves, Stefan and Carol S. Carson. "*Offshore Financial Center Program: A Progress Report." Prepared by the Monetary and Exchange Affairs and Statistics Departments*, International Monetary Fund (March 2003).

Institute of International Bankers. *Global Survey 2003*. New York: Institute of International Bankers, 2003.

International Monetary Fund. *Offshore Financial Centers (OFCs)*. Washington, D.C.: International Monetary Fund, mimeo, 2000.

International Monctary Fund. *International Capital Markets*. Washington, D.C.: International Monetary Fund, 2001.

James, Christopher. "Some Evidence on the Uniqueness of Bank Loans." *Journal of Financial Economics* 19 (December 1987): 217-235.

John, Kose, Teresa A. John and Anthony Saunders. "Universal Banking and Firm Risk Taking." *Journal of Banking and Finance* 18 (January 1994): 307-323.

Kane, Edward J. "Designing Financial Safety Nets to Fit Country Circumstances." World Bank Policy Research Working Paper No. 2453 (2000).

Kang, Jun-Koo and René M. Stulz. "Do Bank Shocks Affect Borrowing Firm Performance? An Analysis of the Japanese Experience." *Journal of Business* 73 (January 2000): 1-23.

Kashyap, Anil K., Jeremy C. Stein, and David W. Wilcox. "Monetary Policy and Credit Conditions: Evidence from the Composition of External Finance." *American Economic Review* 83 (March 1993): 78-98.

Kashyap, Anil K. and Jeremy C. Stein. "What Do a Million Observations on Banks Say about the Transmission of Monetary Policy?" *American Economic Review* 90 (June 2000): 407-428.

Khan, Aubhik. "The Finance and Growth Nexus." *Business Review*, Federal Reserve Bank of Philadelphia (January/February 2000).

Khan, Mohsin S. and Abdelhak S. Senhadj. "Financial Development and Economic Growth: An Overview" IMF Working Paper, International Monetary Fund, WP/00/209, (December 2000).

King, Robert G. and Ross Levine. "Finance and Growth: Schumpeter Might Be Right." *Quarterly Journal of Economics* 108 (1993): 717-737.

King, Robert G. and Ross Levine. "Finance, Entrepreneurship, and Growth." *Journal of Monetary Economics* 32 (December 1993b): 513-542.

La Porta, Rafael, Florencio Lopez-de-Silanes, Andrei Shleifer and Robert W. Vishny. "Law and Finance." *Journal of Political Economy* 106 (December 1998): 1113-1155.

Lannoo, Karel. "*Challenges to the Structure of Financial Supervision in the EU.*" CEPS Working Party Report, Centre for European Policy Studies, (Chairman: David Green), (July 2000).

Levine, Ross. "Financial Development and Economic Growth: Views and Agenda." *Journal of Economic Literature* 35 (June 1997): 688-726.

Levine, Ross. "The Legal Environment, Banks, and Long-Run Economic Growth." *Journal of Money, Credit, and Banking* 30, Part II (August 1998): 596-613.

Levine, Ross, Norman Loayza and Thorsten Beck. "Financial Intermediation and Growth: Causality and Causes." *Journal of Monetary Economics* 46 (August 2000): 31-77.

Macey, Jonathan R. and Maureen O'Hara. "The Corporate Governance of Banks." *Economic Policy Review*, Federal Reserve Bank of New York 9, Special Issue (April 2003): 91-108.

Martínez, José de Luna and Thomas A. Rose. "International Survey of Integrated Supervision," in *Financial Regulation: A Guide to Structural Reform*, ed. Douglas Arner and Jan-Juy Lin, 3-39. Hong Kong: Sweet & Maxwell Asia, 2003.

McKinnon, Ronald I. *Money and Capital in Economic Development*. Washington, DC: Brookings Institution, 1973.

Mester, Loretta J. "What Is the Point of Credit Scoring?" *Business Review*, Federal Reserve Bank of Philadelphia (June 1997): 449-470.

Office of the Comptroller of the Currency. *Detecting Red Flags in Board Reports: A Guide for Directors*. Washington, D.C.: Office of the Comptroller of the Currency, 2003.

Ongena, Steven, David C. Smith and Dag Michalsen. "Firms and Their Distressed Banks: Lessons from the Norwegian Banking Crisis." *Journal of Financial Economics* 67 (January 2003): 81-112.

Palia, Darius and Robert Porter. "Contemporary Issues in Regulatory Risk Management of Commercial Banks." *Financial Markets, Institutions & Instruments* 12 (September 2003): 223-289. Malden, MA: Blackwell Publishing Inc.

Peek, Joe and Eric S. Rosengren. "Collateral Damage: Effects of the Japanese Bank Crisis on Real Activity in the United States." *American Economic Review* 90 (March 2000): 30-45.

Phumiwasana, Triphon. "*Financial Structure, Economic Growth and Stability*." Ph.D. diss., Claremont Graduate University, Department of Economics, 2003.

Quintyn, Marc G. and Michael W. Taylor. "*Regulatory and Supervisory Independence and Financial Stability*." IMF Working Paper, International Monetary Fund (January 2002).

Rajan, Raghuram G. "Insider and Outsiders, the Choice Between Informed and Arm's Length Debt." *Journal of Finance* 47 (September 1992): 1367-1400.

Rajan, Raghuram G. and Luigi Zingales. "Financial Dependence and Growth" *American Economic Review* 88 (June 1998): 559-586.

Rule, David. "The Credit Derivatives Market: Its Development and Possible Implications for Financial Stability." *Financial Stability Review* 10 (June 2001): 117-140.

Saunders, Anthony. "Banking and Commerce: An Overview of the Public Policy Issues." *Journal of Banking and Finance* 18 (January 1994): 231-254.

Saunders, Anthony and Linda Allen. *Credit Risk Measurement: New Approaches to Value at Risk and Other Paradigms*, 2nd ed. New York: John Wiley & Sons, Inc., 2002.

Sharpe, Steven A. "Asymmetric Information, Bank Lending and Implicit Contracts: A Stylized Model of Customer Relationships." *Journal of Finance* 45 (August 1990):1069-1087.

Shleifer, Andrei and Robert W. Vishny. "A Survey of Corporate Governance." *Journal of Finance* 52 (June 1997): 737-783.

Schüler, Martin. "*How Do Banking Supervisors Deal with Europe-wide Systemic Risk.*" Discussion Paper No. 03-03, Centre for European Economic Research (2003).

Slovin, Myron B., Marie E. Sushka and John A. Poloncheck. "The Value of Bank Durability: Borrowers as Bank Stakeholders." *Journal of Finance* 48 (March 1993): 274-266

Stiglitz, Joseph and Andrew Weiss. "Incentive Effects of Terminations: Applications to the Credit and Labor Markets." *American Economic Review* 73 (December 1983): 912-927.

Sundararajan, V., David Marston, and Ritu Basu. "Financial System Standards and Financial Stability - The Case of Basel Core Principles." IMF Working Paper No. 01/62 (May 2001).

Suss, Esther C., Oral H. Williams, and Chandima Mendis. "*Caribbean Offshore Financial Centers: Past, Present and Possibilities for the Future,*" IMF Working Paper (May 2002).

Wachtel, Paul. "*How Much Do We Really Know about Growth and Finance*?" *Economic Review*, Federal Reserve Bank of Atlanta (1st Quarter 2003): 33-57.

World Trade Organization. *General Agreement on Trade in Services*. Geneva, Switzerland: World Trade Organization. *http://www.wto.org/english/res_e/booksp_e/analytic_index_e/gats_e.htm.*

INDEX